THE

Before-You-Marry
BOOK *of* QUESTIONS

THE

Before-You-Marry

BOOK *of* QUESTIONS

BILL & PAM FARREL

HARVEST HOUSE PUBLISHERS
EUGENE, OREGON

This book contains stories in which the author has changed people's names and some details of their situations in order to protect their privacy.

Cover design by Left Coast Design, Portland, Oregon

Cover photo © bluehand / Shutterstock

The authors are represented by the literary agency of Alive Communications, Inc., 7680 Goddard Street, Suite 200, Colorado Springs, CO 80920. www.alivecommunications.com.

THE BEFORE-YOU-MARRY BOOK OF QUESTIONS
Copyright © 2013 by Bill and Pam Farrel
Published by Harvest House Publishers
Eugene, Oregon 97402
www.harvesthousepublishers.com

Library of Congress Cataloging-in-Publication Data
    Farrel, Bill, 1959-
    The before-you-marry book of questions / Bill and Pam Farrel.
        pages cm
    ISBN 978-0-7369-5147-0 (pbk.)
    ISBN 978-0-7369-5148-7 (eBook)
    1. Marriage—Religious aspects—Christianity—Miscellanea. 2. Weddings—Planning—Miscellanea. I. Title.
    BV835.F36 2013
    248.8'44—dc23
                                                              2013022699

Printed in the United States of America
            13 14 15 16 17 18 19 20 21 22 / BP-JH / 10 9 8 7 6 5 4 3 2 1

He who finds a wife finds what is good
And receives favor from the LORD.
(Proverbs 18:22)

To our daughters-in-love,
Hannah and Caleigh.
We prayed for each of you before you were even conceived.
You are so perfect for each of our sons,
who were wise enough to marry you.
And after raising three sons,
it is so much fun to have two more "Mrs. Farrels" in the clan!

To the couples who have given Bill the honor
of performing your wedding ceremony,
thanks for sharing this journey of love.
Other couples will be strengthened
because of the wisdom God imparted in our times together.

Acknowledgments

Lots of *thank-yous*! to Bob Hawkins Jr. and the
wonderful Harvest House Publishers' team.

Overwhelming gratitude to Rod Morris, our amazing
editor of extreme patience, talent, and wit.

Very heartfelt appreciation to our marriage mentors—the Conways, the Wilcoxes, the Bucks, the
O'Neals—who shared their insights and time to
make us wiser so we can help others.

Extreme gratefulness to our married children, especially our sons, who have been used as examples in
book after book, year after year. Guys, thanks for
living a life of integrity, like an open book, so others can gain from your authenticity.

Contents

Are You Ready for Love?

Decide to Be Relationship Ready

May the most you wish for
Be the least you get. [1]

 $\mathcal{Y}$ ou picked up this book because you are in love (or you hope to be in love)! Love matters to you. You might also want to read this book because you want the best life has to offer and you know that experiencing real love is a big part of what makes for a happy life. You also might be holding this book because you have been hurt by love and you never want to experience that kind of pain again. Or you might simply have a lot of questions about love:

- How can I tell if I am in love?
- What is healthy love?
- Is there such a thing as love at first sight?
- Can love last a lifetime?
- Can I heal my broken heart and find love again?
- How do I navigate love and move a relationship forward in a positive way?
- How can I get better at falling in love with the right person?

- What are the things that blow love apart and how can I avoid them?
- How do I know that this is "the one"?
- What is the next step in love?
- Should I marry?

We want to help you explore those questions—and more! Love uncovers lots of questions within us because it is a journey of self-discovery driven forward by curiosity. As you read, we are confident we have questions to add you might not even have thought about asking yet.

The Original Love

We often have some unique views on love from childhood, like those from these kids:

"Love is when a girl puts on perfume and a boy puts on shaving cologne and they go out and smell each other."—Karl, age 5

"Love is when you go out to eat and give somebody most of your french fries without making them give you any of theirs."—Chrissy, age 6

"Love is what makes you smile when you're tired."—Terri, age 4

"Love is when my mommy makes coffee for my daddy and she takes a sip before giving it to him, to make sure the taste is OK."—Danny, age 7

"Love is when you kiss all the time. Then when you get tired of kissing, you still want to be together and you talk more. My Mommy and Daddy are like that. They look gross when they kiss."—Emily, age 8

"Love is what's in the room with you at Christmas if you stop opening presents and listen."—Bobby, age 7

"Love is when you tell a guy you like his shirt, then he wears it every day."—Noelle, age 7

"Love is like a little old woman and a little old man who are still friends even after they know each other so well."—Tommy, age 6

"Love is when Mommy gives Daddy the best piece of chicken."—Elaine, age 5

"Love is when Mommy sees Daddy smelly and sweaty and still says he is handsomer than a movie star."—Chris, age 7

"When you love somebody your eyelashes go up and down and little stars come out of you."—Karen, age 7 [2]

The View from the One Who Knows Love Best

Let's begin by looking at love by the one who created love—God. How do we know God originated love?

And so we know and rely on the love God has for us. *God is love.* Whoever lives in love lives in God, and God in them (1 John 4:16 emphasis added).

We love because he first loved us (1 John 4:19).

When the Bible says, "God is love," it means that love is the driving force of his character. Everything he does, everything he creates, everything he communicates stems from his love. Out of his desire for us to experience the fullness of life, he "cloned" love, making it available for all the humans he created out of his love. Since he is the creator of love, any time your love for one another aligns with God's principles, it will run smoother, work better, feel richer, be kinder, and have a sweeter influence on others. We can bank on this love. First John 4:16 says we "know" and "rely on" the love God has for us. "Know" means we grasp it with our minds, and "rely on" means we embrace it in our hearts. God's love is intellectually and emotionally faithful.

It Is All Good!

A very interesting word is repeated throughout the creation account in Genesis:

When God created light, *"God saw that the light was good"* (Genesis 1:3-4).

When he created the land and sea, *"God saw that it was good"* (1:9-10).

When he created vegetation, *"God saw that it was good"* (1:11-12).

When he created the sun and moon, *"God saw that it was good"* (1:16-18).

When he created the animals, *"God saw that it was good"* (1:20-25).

After creating Adam and assigning him work, God said, "It is *not good* for the man to be alone" (2:18a). Then he created Eve as a suitable helper (2:18b) and "God saw all that he had made, and *it was very good*" (1:31).

The word translated "good" is the Hebrew word *tôb*, which means "beautiful or functioning the way God intended." "Good," in this context, describes the ability of God's creation to function in the way he intended it to operate. The modifier "very" applies words such as *abundantly, exceedingly, immensely,* or *intensely* to the functionality of what God created. So marriage, the uniting of a man and a woman in love, is abundantly, exceedingly, utterly, immensely beautiful!

As a result, many synonyms are used to describe goodness in relationships:

Desirable	*Favorable*
Beautiful	*Precious*
Moral	*Pure*
Happy	*Right*
Delightful	*Worthy*

These same words are often used to describe how we feel when we are in love and about the one we love. One of the main questions, therefore, that helps evaluate whether a relationship has what it takes for a lifetime of love is, "Does our relationship function the way God intended to the point that it can be called good?"

To say the least, God has a very high (on the highest end of any scale) view of love and marriage. Therefore, to keep things *tôb* or beautiful in a love relationship, it is wise to listen to God's opinions on how relationship, love, marriage, sex, and intimacy work.

The Beautiful Life

We have always encouraged people to build a life worthy of inviting someone into. When you build your own life to be *tôb* or beautiful, you will attract others who also want life and love to be *tôb* or beautiful. Quality attracts quality. Healthy attracts healthy.

We recommend you take some time right now to work through the following self-evaluation exercise. In each area of your life listed below, place an *X* on the line to indicate how *tôb* (how beautiful, healthy, right, good) you think you are in this area. No one will be "very *tôb*" in every area. Notice the last question is to rate how honest you have been in your answers. In relationships, honesty is very *tôb*.

Emotional: Are you stable psychologically and socially? Do people, especially leaders and peers, see you as a stable, loving, caring, and well-adjusted person?

NOT TÔB   VERY TÔB

GOAL: Change I would like to make to become more *tôb* (beautiful/excellent) in this area: I need to respect my self as God sees me

Intellectual: Are you willing to grow in your knowledge about how relationships work and the skills that lead to lifelong, healthy love?

NOT TÔB VERY TÔB

GOAL: Change I would like to make to become more *tôb* (beautiful/excellent) in this area:

Vocational: Is your work and career life on track? (If you are in college or receiving training, can you see the end in sight and have a career direction in mind?)

NOT TÔB VERY TÔB

GOAL: Change I would like to make to become more *tôb* (beautiful/excellent) in this area:

Relational: Have you dealt with any past ghosts from your family of origin or past relationships? Is your heart healed, soft, and positive toward love and relationship?

NOT TÔB VERY TÔB

GOAL: Change I would like to make to become more *tôb* (beautiful/excellent) in this area:

Spiritual: Are you seeking answers to your spiritual questions? Are you growing in your love and knowledge of God? Are you connected to people who can help you learn more about God and how he views love and relationships?

NOT TÔB   VERY TÔB

GOAL: Change I would like to make to become more *tôb* (beautiful/excellent) in this area:

I need some mentors to help me.

Physical: Are you fit and healthy (or working at being this way), and do you care about your appearance?

NOT TÔB   VERY TÔB

GOAL: Change I would like to make to become more *tôb* (beautiful/excellent) in this area:

I need to take care of my weight

Inspirational: Do you serve God, church, nonprofits, your community, neighbors? How other-centered are you?

NOT TÔB   (VERY TÔB)

GOAL: Change I would like to make to become more *tôb* (beautiful/excellent) in this area:

Financial: Are you earning, saving, and spending money in a way to stabilize and provide for your life today and prepare well for tomorrow?

NOT TÔB   VERY TÔB

GOAL: Change I would like to make to become more *tôb* (beautiful/excellent) in this area:

need to save

Truthful: How honest, straightforward, and authentic have you been in your answers?

NOT TÔB   VERY TÔB

GOAL: Change I would like to make to become more *tôb* (beautiful/excellent) in this area:

Relationship Ready?

In *Not Another Dating Book: A Devotional Guide to All Your Relationships*, Renee Fisher gives some good common-sense advice:

> Honesty is so crucial to strong relationships. And not just honesty about the "big stuff" like past relationships. Be honest about your future. Be honest about your weaknesses. Be honest about your hopes, your regrets, and your fears. Honesty up front will prevent heartbreak later. [3]

To be honest with another, you first need to be honest with yourself. Take time to look at how ready you are for a future relationship by how healed you are from any past ones. Renee continues,

How can you offer your whole self to a person if your heart still belongs to someone else? How can you fully embrace and rejoice in a new relationship if you are still licking old wounds? It is not fair to you or to the new person in your life. [4]

In *Single Men Are Like Waffles, Single Women Are Like Spaghetti*, we have an entire chapter devoted to help people become more relationship ready, but here is a quick checklist. Do a quick inventory and see just how ready you might be for a more serious relationship that is leading to marriage:

Are You Ready?

- Have you been on your own? (Are you paying for your own housing, food, personal items, car, phone, insurance? Are you responsible for your own personal decisions, schedule, life plan?)

- Are you out of debt or have you implemented a plan to consistently reduce your debt and pay off loans?

- Do you have a strong plan and direction for your life?

- Do you have a job and career and have you seen any success in this, or do you have a clear path to college or grad school graduation?

- Do you have a dependable, authentic group of friends you can confide in and trust their opinions and counsel?

- Do you have a healthy relationship with your parents, grandparents, and extended family—or have you sought to have one from your side of the relationship?

- Have you dealt with your family-of-origin issues? Did either of your parents have addictions, abandon you, abuse you, and so on? Have you pursued counseling or mentoring to overcome those hurts?

- Have you acknowledged and forgiven any hurts from past relationships?

- Have you dealt with any of your demons (drugs, drinking, pornography, sexual promiscuity, gambling, or shopping addictions)?

- Have you finished and closed the doors on all past relationships? (You are not seeing a person from your past or carrying romantic feelings for him or her.)

- If you were previously married, have you completed all details of that relationship? Is the divorce *final* (you're not just separated)? If children are involved, has a custody settlement been agreed upon? Have you divided property?

- If you were in a serious dating relationship, a previous engagement, or marriage, have you given yourself time to regroup and readjust to life as a solo person? (One healthy time gauge would be *at least* one month off *all* dating relationships for each year you were with a person. For example, if you dated for two years, were engaged a year, and then broke it off, you should not go on any kind of date for at least three months. Most people require double this (so six-months breathing room). If you lived with someone or a marriage ended, you should double this again. So if you dated two years, were engaged one, and married for three, at minimum give yourself a year or even two to recover or regroup.

- If you have children, are they at a place they can handle change or a new person entering your life? (Kids are *not* as resilient as you might want them to be. It is wise to consult a licensed counselor who specializes in children before exposing your children to romantic relationships. Use the wisdom of those who have a proven track record of helping children and families to add to your own wisdom before making life-altering decisions.)

- Do you have a growing relationship with God in a way that you can sense when God is leading and guiding your life?

You should have been able to mark off all the items on this list, and if you were not, then those are areas you will want to make forward movement on before jumping into a serious dating relationship, engagement, or marriage. A healthy person is not afraid of self-assessment and self-improvement because they see the value of becoming their best for the sake of all those they love, including the one they will marry. Things do not need to be perfect, but from your side of any and all relationships, have you tried to make things right?

Time to Reflect

HIS Perspective

Looking at your list of how *tôb* your life is and the goals you've laid out to live more as God intended, how ready are you for marriage? Is there any area you need to refine, any skeletons in the closet you need to address, or any areas you need some time to work on so that your life is a stronger one to invite someone you love into? Take time to write down your thoughts and feelings as you reflect on this list of life responsibilities on your journey toward *tôb* or the "beautiful life" God has in mind for you.

Perspective

Looking at your list of how *tôb* your life is and the goals you've laid out to live more as God intended, how ready are you for marriage? Is there any area you need to refine, any skeletons in the closet you need to address, or any areas you need some time to work on so that your life is a stronger one to invite someone you love into? Take time to write down your thoughts and feelings as you reflect on this list of life responsibilities on your journey toward *tôb* or the "beautiful life" God has in mind for you.

Marriage as God Intended

When God created Adam, he connected earth to heaven vertically. When he created the first marriage, he connected a man and a woman in a horizontal relationship (one that many describe as "heaven on earth").

Let's look at what we can learn about love, marriage, sex, and relationships from the creation story in Genesis 2:

> This is the account of the heavens and the earth when they were created, when the LORD God made the earth and the heavens.
>
> Now no shrub had yet appeared on the earth and no plant had yet sprung up, for the LORD God had not sent rain on the earth and there was no one to work the ground, but streams came up from the earth and watered the whole surface of the ground. Then the LORD God formed a man

from the dust of the ground and breathed into his nostrils the breath of life, and the man became a living being.

Now the LORD God had planted a garden in the east, in Eden; and there he put the man he had formed. The LORD God made all kinds of trees grow out of the ground—trees that were pleasing to the eye and good for food. In the middle of the garden were the tree of life and the tree of the knowledge of good and evil.

A river watering the garden flowed from Eden...

The LORD God took the man and put him in the Garden of Eden to work it and take care of it. And the LORD God commanded the man, "You are free to eat from any tree in the garden; but you must not eat from the tree of the knowledge of good and evil, for when you eat from it you will certainly die."

The LORD God said, "It is not good for the man to be alone. I will make a helper suitable for him."

Now the LORD God had formed out of the ground all the wild animals and all the birds in the sky. He brought them to the man to see what he would name them; and whatever the man called each living creature, that was its name. So the man gave names to all the livestock, the birds in the sky and all the wild animals.

But for Adam no suitable helper was found. So the LORD God caused the man to fall into a deep sleep; and while he was sleeping, he took one of the man's ribs and then closed up the place with flesh. Then the LORD God made a woman from the rib he had taken out of the man, and he brought her to the man.

The man said,

> "This is now bone of my bones
>   and flesh of my flesh;

> she shall be called 'woman,'
>   for she was taken out of man."

That is why a man leaves his father and mother and is united to his wife, and they become one flesh.

Adam and his wife were both naked, and they felt no shame (Genesis 2:4-25).

This is the account of the creation of the first man and woman and of their marriage as God intended, before they decided they had a better plan than God. It has been said there is a reason life in the garden was so perfect: Adam and Eve had the perfect marriage because he didn't have to hear about all the men she could have married, and she didn't have to hear about the way his mother cooked!

Okay, joking aside, God's original plan and intent for marriage was pretty amazing, as we see demonstrated in the following five principles.

Principle 1: Man and Woman Were Made for Loyalty

God formed a man from the dust of the ground and breathed into his nostrils the breath of life, and that is what turned Adam into a living being. Dirt (made by God) + God's breath = Life. Yes, we'd say we can trace human life back to some God "DNA." We are an authentic reflection of the divine. In Genesis 1:27, remember, it was clearly stated,

> God created mankind in his own image,
>   in the image of God he created them;
>   male and female he created them.

Because we were all made as a likeness, model, or replica of God's heart and character, we have intrinsic value. When you are loyal to another, you look for ways to recognize, applaud, and promote this value. When loyalty is a conviction in your heart, traits such as respect, honor, taking the high road, integrity, honesty, and truthfulness will become pervasive aspects of your interaction with the opposite sex.

This is countercultural in today's world. Music, movies, and modern art are just a few of the places where infidelity, fornication, and illicit sex are elevated. We have nicknames for the sexually experienced that have evolved into compliments from the scandalous definitions your parents or grandparents understood them to be. The media tosses out "player" and "playboy" as some kind of sought after title or trophy. The Urban Dictionary allows people to add their own definitions of words, and some of these are closer to reality when describing a "playa" as a guy who:

- Doesn't understand the meaning of relationship.
- Is in full reproductive mode.
- Is very good at making girls think he is into them (and very proficient at breaking said girls' hearts).
- Is maintaining supposedly exclusive relationships with multiple girls simultaneously.
- Lies often, not only about his other relationships, but about himself, his daily life, and false promises. He will try to manage several relationships, but is basically only in them to get some sort of sexual pleasure.

Urban slang calls a female "playa" a slut. One definition included, "She probably is not in a relationship, and she equalizes herself to guys by treating sex the same way they do." It would not be alarming if these descriptions acted as a warning to people to avoid unhealthy relationships. Instead, the trend is toward friends with benefits, casual sex despite the rise of sexually transmitted diseases, and cohabitation without commitment. Rather than promoting the limitless value of each other, culture is spiraling down to the lowest common denominator as it sets people up for all kinds of hurt and pain when it comes to "love."

However, because you picked up this book, you likely have the foresight to see that selfish, shortsighted relationship choices lead only to disappointment, broken hearts, and self-defeating habits.

We have definitely lost our way as a society when it comes to trivializing and devaluing sexuality as a gift, intended by God for marriage. One girl in Norway had a male friend who was interested in her romantically—he wanted to have sex with her—but she thought of him as "just a friend" and said, "Only if you can get one million 'Likes' on Facebook—then I'd have sex with you." Well, he posted a photo with the bet on his Facebook page asking people to "like him." People around the world responded and sent it to friends. More than one million responded! He told his local press that having achieved his goal, the two of them have decided to "keep what we promised." [5] Really? Sex as a game? A bet? A Facebook post? How extremely shallow and devoid of meaning.

God calls us to take a higher road than this. He protects the heart, provides a future, and pumps power into our character so we can live out a love much more meaningful, virtuous, and real. God offers simple insights that make all relationships work, and one of the goals of this book is to help you be a hero in love and create an epic love story—one that will be passed down from generation to generation and build strength into your family tree.

HIS Perspective

When I (Bill) was a kid, I wanted to be a superhero. I looked up to Batman, Superman, Aquaman, the Flash, the Green Hornet, and other "marvel" wonders. I wanted to be heroic like they were. There seemed to be something almost Herculean about rescuing a damsel in distress or overcoming seemingly insurmountable odds in the name of love. But then I heard about Jesus and read his words, "Greater love has no one than this: to lay down one's life…" (John 15:13).

Take time to write some bullet points or a paragraph or two that describe what you consider "heroic love." What does it look like? What would a hero do for the love of his life? Heroes often protect from harm or rescue from evil, so what would that look like to you in daily life, in a relationship with someone you say you love?

Her Perspective

Some women in history are seen as heroines: Deborah in the Bible rode into battle next to the general to ensure victory (see Judges 4 and 5). In legend, perhaps a warrior-princess like Xena, fighting for the greater good, would be a heroine to you. In literature, maybe Katniss of *The Hunger Games* comes to mind because of her willingness to give her life in place of another.

Or maybe someone like Clara Barton is where your mind goes. She was the nurse who risked her life on the front lines to bandage the wounded during the Civil War and who launched the American Red Cross. Or perhaps a leader of the people like Golda Meir of Israel or Margaret Thatcher of Great Britain, women who rose in power by looking out for the needs of the people, is how you would picture heroic.

What does it mean to be a heroine in a love relationship? Write down some thoughts in a paragraph or two and describe a heroic love.

Love Chat

If you are in an exclusive dating relationship, set a time to read your descriptions of heroic love to each other. After your date has read their journal entry, tell them how you feel about their images of what is heroic in love. Each of you take time to complete these sentences:

When I think of couples who had "heroic love," people that come to mind are_____

_____

In my own family or friendship circle, people that I think love heroically are_____

because_____

Before I met you, the time in my life that I most needed a hero was

_____

I think what I was looking for or needed was_____

_____

The part of your description of being a hero in love that most reso-
nated with me or that meant the most to me was_____

_____

because_____

_____

If you have been dating a while and are headed toward engagement
or are already engaged, then add in this sentence:

A time I felt heroic love from you was_____

_____

and it made me feel_____

_____

Principle 2: Man and Woman Were Made for Harmony

Marriage was made *before* the fall. The garden was a good environment. "You complete me" has become a popular love line and, in
a sense, this is biblically accurate. Genesis 2:18 says, "The LORD God
said, 'It is not good for the man to be alone. I will make a helper suitable for him.'"

God says it is *not tôb*—not good, beautiful, or as God intended—
for man to be "alone," to be in solitude, separated, apart, isolated,
and curtained off. It is pretty clear that, for the vast majority, God
intended man to live with woman in a committed, monogamous, love
relationship.

The exceptions are those who have been given a gift of singleness.
As Paul says to the church in Corinth, "But each of you has your own
gift from God…Now to the unmarried and the widows I say: It is good

for them to stay unmarried, as I do. But if they cannot control themselves, they should marry, for it is better to marry than to burn with passion" (1 Corinthians 7:7-9). Singleness is a gift that enables a person to focus fully on service to God and not have to balance work, marriage, and family. You probably got this book because singleness is not a gift God gave you, and that is not surprising since he designed the majority of us for marriage.

The term translated as "suitable" in Genesis 2:18 is a unique term. It literally means "according to the opposite of him," and is variously translated as "suitable," "fit," "just right," and "corresponding." In context it is the complete picture of God making all the animals, parading the animals past Adam, and Adam realizing he is alone (and that is not *tôb*). As Adam saw each animal with its partner, he became aware that his partner was missing.

God then removed one of Adam's ribs and made Eve for Adam. We have a fond affection for this term *make*. It is much more than make cookies or make dinner or make a date. *Make* (*banah*) is a much more personal term here. It means God built Eve. He planned out her design. He assembled her characteristics in precise order. He carefully put the finishing touches on her so she was exactly matched to her purpose. *Make* can also mean "to accomplish, appoint, or bring forth." So God didn't just dream about Eve; he accomplished the dream.

You are certainly free to decide on your own who you want to marry, but it is good to remember that you have a powerful advocate in your pursuit. God knows who has the characteristics that best complement your life. In his love and creativity, he has created someone who fits in your life and will help you become a better person. When you discover another who was designed for you by God, life feels more complete and your relationship is infused with a strong sense of honor.

I (Pam) remember holding the face of my daughter-in-law framed by her wedding veil, looking in her eyes and saying, "I prayed for my son's future wife since before he was even born. I asked God to bring him the perfect woman who was made just right for him. I also asked God to prepare my son so he would be just right for her. God answered my prayers! But even more, God answered my son's prayers when God formed you. The Bible says you are wonderfully and beautifully made. I thank God because you are a gift to my son and you are a gift to our family."

As I was praying with the bride, her mother was telling my son the same thing! Be assured, God is a personal God. If you listen, walk closely with him, and follow his lead, he will faithfully lead you to the mate he fashioned for you.

Principle 3: Man and Woman Were Made for Synergy

Here's a news flash: we were designed to *work* together in marriage even though so much of dating is playing, fun, and celebration. Real love thrives in real life so it is important to learn how to work as a team in the days after you say, "I do." God clearly explained that Adam was to work by tending the garden. The work was large, so God made a helper designed to assist, serve, strengthen, and support in a way that they could accomplish more together than they could as individuals.

One of our favorite sections in most of the wedding ceremonies we have been involved with reads:

> Woman was not taken from man's head to rule over him, nor from his feet to be trampled upon by him, but from his side that she might be his equal, from under his arm that she might receive his protection, and from near his heart that she might own and command his love.

Beautiful sentiment, right? It's poetic and profound as it calls all of us to a life of teamwork. The wife was not made to be a servant like a maid. Rather she was to be a vital teammate with her husband to create a legacy in their family and to invest in their community.

We believe every marriage is a unique creation of God in the same way that every individual is unique. This uniqueness includes the way you interact with each other and how you treat each other, but it also extends to the purpose that brought you together. You may be able to clearly state that purpose or it may be a mystery to you, but part of what brought you together is a shared sense of the direction you are supposed to be heading in life. This can be one of the best ways to know if a potential spouse is "right for you." If you sense you can give God greater glory as a united team, and that your love will influence more people than your individual efforts, your confidence level can rise in moving forward in the relationship. To help you clarify your ability to pursue a common purpose, write your response to the following:

My purpose in life, as I understand it today, is:_____
_____
_____

Evidence I see that my romantic interest shares this purpose includes:
_____
_____

I have the following strengths:_____
_____
_____

These strengths complement my romantic interest in the following ways:_____
_____

My romantic interest has the following strengths:_____
_____
_____

These strengths compensate for the weaknesses in my life in the following ways:_____
_____

Principle 4: Man and Woman Were Made for Monogamy

God designed marriage as a covenant relationship between one man and one woman. Look at the pattern in Genesis. God made a man and created a woman for him. He planted within them both the potential to multiply. The sperm or seed in the man was designed to be united with an egg from the woman God designed for him. Holy matrimony is like a creative textual equation: 1 man + 1 woman 2gether 4 Life = gr8 marriage. Look around the garden. There were no other men or women. One man and one woman united to become one flesh. In a sense, God performed the first wedding ceremony when he created these two, introduced them, and then gave them a vision for their life and future.

When God formed Eve, he first took a rib from Adam and then closed him back up. He didn't keep creating women. He gave Adam one wife. He gave Eve one husband. Before sin entered, when Eve and Adam rebelled against God's plan, monogamy for a lifetime was God's intention. Think of it. God designed Adam and Eve to be skilled lovers who could encourage and support each other for a lifetime. Their choice to ignore God's plan complicated everything for all of us, but it doesn't change the fact that one of life's great accomplishments is to become skilled lovers who can encourage and support each other throughout our earthly journey. Monogamy is *tôb* because it is beautiful as God intended.

Principle 5: Man and Woman Were Made for Intimacy

After the author of Genesis describes the creation of Eve from the rib of Adam, he concludes, "That is why a man leaves his father and mother and is united to his wife, and they become one flesh" (Genesis 2:24). Ever since, a husband and wife form one family, establish one system for raising kids, become known as one unit, and become one physically through sexual intercourse. The result is they end up sharing all of life with each other.

In our book *Red-Hot Monogamy*, we explain that to truly be intimate, you have to seek to be on the same page with your spouse in eight important areas:

- Social
- Financial
- Recreational
- Vocational
- Parental
- Emotional
- Spiritual
- Sexual

This does not mean you are clones of each other, but it does mean you share a common value system when it comes to these vital life components. If one of you believes money should be earned by hard work and the other thinks the government should take care of you, then there will be discord. If one of you believes in being consistent with parental discipline while the other believes the child should call the shots, there will be discord. Where there is discord, there is not a lot of "red-hot monogamy." Where there is discord, your marriage is not a very bright light, not an accurate reflection of God's love and commitment to reach the heart of people. This is why God challenges us, "Do not be bound together with unbelievers; for what partnership have righteousness and lawlessness, or what fellowship has light with darkness?" (2 Corinthians 6:14 NASB). God wants to protect people's marriages from discord, frustration, and disharmony so we can enjoy consistent intimacy in the vital areas of life.

If you have romantic feelings for someone who is not a believer and follower of Christ, we hope you will stop and ask yourself, *Why do I want to connect my heart to someone who does not share my faith?* It is not that you are better because you believe in Jesus, but it does mean you are following different life paths. If you stay on this path of entwining your lives, you will eventually face a fork in the road that will break your heart. Your value systems will come in conflict on some of your most important decisions. Your influence on your kids will be at odds with each other in some of the most sensitive issues. Your love for Jesus will be challenged, and you will be tempted to compromise your faith for the sake of reducing conflict. God is not trying to make your life harder. Rather, he is trying to guide you away from disappointment, heartache, and frustration.

It's the same way in love. If you want a sex life that is red-hot, you have to be able to trust each other. You can ignore almost anything early in a relationship, but as time passes your ability to trust one another will determine the quality of your sex life. If you agree on decisions regarding finances, social commitments, parental strategies, you will conclude you have chosen well and have a great team. In this atmosphere, sexual intimacy is consistently desirable. When you disagree and argue over the areas of life that are closest to your heart, sexual intimacy begins to feel more like a responsibility than a journey.

You marry who you date, so when you begin a friendship with someone, have your faith-and-values conversation early in your relationship. If the other person does not share your faith, they can remain in your friendship circle but not as a romantic partner, unless they too decide to move under God's umbrella of blessing and begin a personal relationship with the God who created them.

In the garden, the two were to be "one flesh." They were naked and not ashamed, and we can be also. We think every couple should have the goal of being unified in such a way that they have great sex for the rest of their lives.

DATE *to* DISCOVER

In each chapter we will give you a date idea that will lead you toward deeper discovery of the person you are dating. It is our hope and prayer that these will also help you decide if the other person is the partner God created for you to spend the rest of your life with so you can give God the greatest glory together.

I (Pam) grew up as a country girl, so nature screams beauty to my heart. For Bill to truly know me, he needed to experience the farm, the country, and nature with me. Bill was an architect major when I met him. In his heart is a desire to build beauty. For me to really value and appreciate Bill, I needed to see his drawings and go to some of the buildings and structures he thought were beautiful.

This chapter has talked a lot about things that are beautiful in love and life. For this "date to discover," each of you pick something or some place that captures what you see as beautiful and share it with each other. Allow the other person to take in your gift of beauty. Then take time to express why you wanted him or her to experience this with you. Ask how they feel about your chosen *tôb* symbol and what they learned about you because you shared this piece of who you are with them.

A Little Adam & Eve Humor

Little Johnny's Sunday school class was learning how God created everything, including human beings. Johnny seemed especially intent when his teachers told him how Eve was created out of one of Adam's ribs.

Later in the week, his mother noticed him lying down as though he were ill, and said, "Johnny, what is the matter?"

"I have a pain in my side," Johnny said. "I think I'm going to have a wife."

Do We Have a Strong Enough Friendship?

Build a Lasting Foundation

> *May there always be work for your hands to do.*
> *May your purse always hold a coin or two.*
> *May the sun always shine upon your window pane.*
> *May a rainbow be certain to follow each rain.*
> *May the hand of a friend always be near to you.*
> *And may God fill your heart with gladness to cheer you.* [1]

*R*omance begins as an intoxicating journey. We have been created in such a way that powerful chemicals get added to the mix when our hearts first get connected to another. Norepinephrine stimulates the production of adrenaline, which causes your heart to race and palms to sweat as you experience an elevated sense of joy and a reduction of appetite. Dopamine elicits elevated feelings of joy, makes us more talkative, and motivates us to express pleasure. Phenylethylamine (PEA) is the trigger that releases both norepinephrine and dopamine while it simultaneously inhibits movement of these chemicals into the bloodstream. The result is they flood the brain with an intoxicating feeling of being in love. [2]

This is why couples newly in love stare at each with a dreamy look in their eyes, have an overstated sense of how wonderful their partner is, and ignore other areas of their life to spend time together. It's also one of the reasons silliness is acceptable when a relationship is new. Young lovers are known to say such things as,

You are the…

- peanut to my butter
- water to my ocean
- glaze on my donut
- spring in my step
- twinkle in my eye
- blue in my sky
- cherry to my sundae

- flip to my flop
- milk to my cookie
- sweet in my dreams
- beat of my heart
- cheese to my macaroni
- best to my friend
- love of my life [3]

Or, "I can conquer the world with one hand as long as you are holding the other." [4]

Most of these sayings are not true—in fact they are not even possible. But they seem appropriate to the emotional climate that develops when PEA is orchestrating your personal concert of obsession with each other.

You want to thoroughly enjoy this chemical kick start to your relationship, but the way you feel early on is not a good indicator of your long-term success. Over time (between six and twenty-four months), the brain grows dull to the effects of these powerful chemicals, which causes the relationship to change. At this point, commitment and friendship between a husband and wife become the glue that holds it all together. Researcher John Gottman has established that couples who are satisfied with their marriages "know each other intimately and are well-versed in each other's likes, dislikes, personality quirks, hopes and dreams. They have an abiding regard for each other and express this fondness in big and little ways." [5] In other words, they are great friends.

So what does it take to build and maintain a friendship that stands the test of time and enhances your life with each passing year?

Will Your Friendship Lower Stress?

It is impossible to be a friend with someone you seldom spend time with. It is also difficult to build a friendship with someone you don't enjoy being around. In the short-term, it is easy to want to be together because you are fascinated with each other and curious about all the new aspects of your relationship. The challenge will come later when responsibility forces you to prioritize your time and stress requires you to do the things that relieve stress effectively. Since a person's spouse will be intricately connected to the responsibility in their family life (careers, bills, kids, home ownership), many couples find that spending time together raises stress over time rather than helping them feel better about themselves and their life. It is vital, therefore, that you discover common interests that will lower stress throughout your journey together.

Take a few minutes to answer the questions below and then honestly share your responses with each other.

 **Perspective**

The areas of my life that tend to increase stress are:

The activities that help lower my stress level are:

The things people do that raise my stress level are:

The things people do that help lower my stress level are:

Perspective

The areas of my life that tend to increase stress are:

The activities that help lower my stress level are:

The things people do that raise my stress level are:

The things people do that help lower my stress level are:

If your friendship is strong enough to navigate the ups and downs of life, there will be some intersection points on your lists of what helps you lower stress. Expect to have differences based on your individual preferences and life experiences, but there should be at least a couple of stress relieving activities you both enjoy. If not, when the inevitable stress mounts, you will isolate yourselves from each other rather than band together as friends to face life together. Based on your responses, are you confident that you can effectively relieve stress as a couple?

Will Your Friendship Welcome Common Struggles?

You are thinking about intimately connecting your life to someone who is as imperfect as you are. You have become skilled at living with your talents and deficiencies because you don't have any other choice. You are aware that you have some unique abilities that are efficient and highly effective in producing results you enjoy. Since these are strong, you rely on them and apply them to life as often as possible.

At the same time, some areas of your life are stubbornly immature. You overreact to some things and cannot give a good reason why. You have habits that improve only a little even when you put enormous amounts of focus and discipline into them. You have attitudes toward certain circumstances and people that are childish. At times you even engage in behavior you instruct other people to avoid.

Real friends commit to accept one another and work through the common struggles of life together. It is even more intense in marriage since you live with this imperfect person every day. You are going to become acutely aware of just how imperfect your loved one is because they are probably strong in areas you are weak and vice versa. Since this is so, it's easy to become critical and demanding in those areas where you are strong and to expect the other person to keep pace. The kind of friendship that makes for great marriages involves a willingness to tackle the common struggles of life together. The question we must all ask is, "Am I willing to be as patient with my partner's growth as I am with my own?" We must then apply the answer to the most common struggles we face, of which there are many. Here are just a few to be aware of:

Premenstrual Syndrome (PMS). Men, the woman you are in love with will wrestle with her menstrual cycle and its effects for the next thirty years or more. She may handle it well or she may get besieged with physical discomfort, emotional turmoil, anxiety, irritability, or dozens of other symptoms. It is best if you can both keep your sense of humor about this one.

> A study conducted by UCLA's Department of Psychiatry has revealed that the kind of face a woman finds attractive on a man can differ depending on where she is in

her menstrual cycle. For example: If she is ovulating, she is attracted to men with rugged and masculine features. However, if she is menstruating or menopausal, she tends to be more attracted to a man with duct tape over his mouth with a spear lodged in his chest and his hair on fire. No further studies are expected.[6]

Male ego. Ladies, the man you are in love with wants to look proficient at all times. He will avoid tasks that he doesn't know how to accomplish and recoil from topics he feels ignorant of. When he gets embarrassed he may become angry, irritable, quiet, withdrawn, demanding, or childish. It is likewise good to cultivate a sense of humor about the male ego because men often misunderstand some of the simplest instructions they receive from the women they love.

This is a story which is perfectly logical to all males:

A wife asks her husband, "Could you please go shopping for me and buy one carton of milk, and if they have eggs, get 6."

A short time later the husband comes back with 6 cartons of milk.

The wife asks him, "Why did you buy 6 cartons of milk?"

He replied, "They had eggs." [7]

In addition to these gender-specific issues, we all struggle to varying degrees with the following inconvenient character traits:

Insecurities, which range from fear of failure to fear of the dark, heights, looking stupid, and on and on the list goes.

Triggers from the past that bring to the surface intense emotions from previous experiences when stimulated by something that is said or done today.

Lust, which tempts men to become obsessed with sexual images and adventures and tempts women to become obsessed with words of love and romance. To be sure, God made us for love, romance, and sex, but we all struggle to keep it in its proper context.

Romantic longings that may raise expectations to a humanly impossible level. For instance, most women dream about their wedding day for years before it actually happens. They imagine what it will be like and build a fantasy image of how beautiful, memorable, and special the day will be. Weddings are great events, but they often fall short of the dream that has been forming in the heart.

Most women have an *ingrained need to connect verbally*. This is based on the fact that the part of her brain that controls verbal interaction is larger than that same part of the brain in men. Early in life, women learn to influence with words and find it to be a powerful tool for connecting with people and getting their way.

Most men want *a relationship that is easy*. They tend to take a simple view of life and learn early they can overpower the situations they care about with strength. They are drawn to building things, athletic pursuits, technology, and projects because there are clear goals, clear procedures, and a clear understanding of when the goal has been reached. They assume relationships will fall in this same category and often get frustrated when they realize it is not true.

Concern over money. We are all emotionally attached to our money, so finances are always a hot topic. Jesus said, "For where your treasure is, there your heart will be also" (Luke 12:34). When you are handling money alone, this tends to not be an issue because you need to negotiate only with yourself. When you connect your money to a spouse, you now have to negotiate with someone who approaches financial matters in a different, but equally emotional, manner as you.

With all of these common struggles, the question becomes, "Are you willing and emotionally mature enough to be sensitive and patient with your loved one's areas of struggle?"

HIS Perspective

Of the common struggles listed above, which one(s) surprised you?

Which of these struggles are you concerned your partner won't be willing to work with?

Which of these struggles are you hoping your partner won't face?

Are there other struggles you face often that are not on the list?

Which of these is so important to you that your partner must accept it, be sensitive about it, and be willing to learn together with you about it?

Perspective

Of the common struggles listed above, which one(s) surprised you?

Which of these struggles are you concerned your partner won't be willing to work with?

Which of these struggles are you hoping your partner won't face?

Are there other struggles you face often that are not on the list?

Which of these is so important to you that your partner must accept it, be sensitive about it, and be willing to learn together with you about it?

Is Your Friendship Based on Loyalty?

In John 15:13, Jesus told his followers, "Greater love has no one than this: to lay down one's life for one's friends." With your true friends, you do what it takes to defend their honor, help them succeed, and protect them from harm. In essence you lay down your life for your friends. Jesus did this for us because he values the relationship. He humbly laid down his glory to experience life on earth just like us. He humbly laid aside his powers to go through the same process of living that we live with. Finally, he humbly laid down his life on the cross so that he might pay the price for our sins, for which we lack sufficient resources to pay (Philippians 2:5-8; 2 Corinthians 5:21; Hebrews 4:15-16).

Loyalty is easy when you agree with everything your girlfriend or boyfriend is doing and they are succeeding and providing new opportunities for you. It is quite another thing when they embarrass you, act foolishly, or take a stand you don't agree with. Keep in mind that we are not talking about the major convictions of life that were addressed in chapter 1 because those profoundly impact the question of whether you should even consider getting married. Here we are talking about personal preferences that help create the emotional and relational atmosphere of your life.

I (Bill) remember the first time Pam's behavior made me uncomfortable around others. At the end of our honeymoon, we traveled to Pam's hometown where her relatives had planned a reception to celebrate our new life together. We ended up spending four days with her mom, brother, and sister. On the third day, Pam started a conflict with her brother. It was over a small thing, and I actually thought her brother was "right." I tried my best to be neutral, but it quickly became obvious I wasn't going to be able to do that. Pam was checking to see who I was most loyal toward. Instead of trying to resolve the issue with everyone involved, I asked Pam to join me in our room so I could reaffirm to her that I was loyal to her. When we were alone, I said, "I don't want to have to choose here between you and your brother, but if I have to choose, I want you to know that I would choose you in a heartbeat." That seemed to be all it took. Suddenly, the friendship was strengthened and the conflict was over.

In addition to behavior in your dating partner that is inconsistent, we live in a world that is critical, immoral, and self-absorbed, so your best friend will be criticized and mistreated. Loyalty will compel you to stand by your friend no matter what. Even when your friend is wrong or deserves the criticism, you will stand together because friendship is stronger than your imperfections.

💜 *Love Chat* 💜

If I disagree with something you have said or done, I will express my loyalty to you by:_____

_____

If you are criticized for something you have said or done, I will express my loyalty to you by:_____

_____

Will Your Loyalty Weather the Seasons of Life?

As you take your marriage journey together, you will go through some distinct stages. Each of these seasons transforms you. The demands placed on you change. The way you allocate your time is unique to each phase. Your energy level and emotional reactions to each phase are different from the phase before. In simplest terms, the major seasons of life include:

Young Adult. This is the time of life before you have children. Life is relatively simple and you have the luxury of focusing on you and your needs. Even if you are married during this time, your life is spontaneous and self-contained. You can go where you want when you want without having to make arrangements for anyone else.

Young Parents. With the birth of your first child, life changes joyfully and dramatically. You rejoice over the new life that has been entrusted to you. Your schedule gets focused around the needs of your young children. Your dignity gets replaced by humility as you change diapers, clean up messes, lose sleep, and give up your free time. You grow stronger and less selfish as a person as you learn to give your life away to others. As the kids grow, you get busier with your career to keep up with the growing needs of your family, and your social life builds around the parents of other kids who are involved in the same activities as your children.

The Oasis. This is the stage where your kids are out of preschool but not yet teens. For the most part, they think Mom and Dad are awesome and wise. They love to hear your ideas and are generally cooperative. However, this is the stage of life when your family pace will pick up as children start various afterschool activities, so as a couple you will need to create a plan to meet the needs of your children and balance that with your need to stay romantically connected.

Parents of Teenagers. Teens have a way of bringing out the best and worst of who you are. You are proud of your kids as they begin to function at a higher level and their giftedness becomes more evident. You also grow irritated with them because they think they are smarter than they actually are and they periodically push you away in an attempt to establish their own identity. You are forced to be secure in your own assessment of your life because your teens tend to be overconfident and overcritical while they express their lack of wisdom.

Midlife/Empty Nesters. At midlife (roughly 45–55), you will do an intense evaluation of yourself. Your body will be changing, and you will realize you cannot rely on sheer strength and tenacity to get things done. You are going to decide if you are willing to switch from a life of productivity to a life of influence. You will have collected significant life experience and have a lot of wisdom to share. This sets you up to be a mentor, advisor, and coach to many others. It is a heavy responsibility, however, so you will need to ask yourself, "Am I willing to share my life experience for the benefit of others?"

Influential Years. On the other side of the midlife evaluation is a life of influence. If you have embraced the challenge and integrated the wisdom of your experience, a new world opens up to you. You are smarter about what you are truly good at and more willing to give it your best effort. You no longer feel a need to do everything and are more content to do what you do best. In addition, others have a natural respect for you because they recognize your insight, confidence, and competence. Others want to learn from you because they recognize you know what you are talking about.

If you have rejected your place of influence, you may become frustrated as you attempt to recapture your younger life. You may become introspective, intensely aware of your personal needs and critical of those who have journeyed with you up to this point.

Mature Years: Eventually, you grow up and have to face the effects of aging. Your body fails to respond as it used to. Health concerns become a greater priority. Activities that used to be easy now take concerted effort, and you may have to take turns being a caretaker for each other. Loyalty tends to be solid at this point because you have been through so much together. We recently experienced this with my (Bill's) parents when they celebrated their sixtieth wedding anniversary.

On their fiftieth, Pam had asked my dad, "What is the secret to staying married to the same woman for fifty years?"

He replied rather quickly, "When we got married, I said, 'For better, for worse.' Most of the time has been worse, but some have been better."

On their sixtieth, Pam repeated the question, "Dad, what is the secret of sixty years?"

This time, he replied tenderly, "I just can't imagine my life without my sweet Betsy."

We encourage you to ask yourselves the following question about your loyalty to each other: "Can I say with full conviction that I will stand by your side through each and every one of these transitions we will go through?"

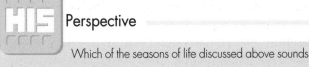

Perspective

Which of the seasons of life discussed above sounds most interesting to you?

Which of the seasons of life makes you nervous?

Perspective

Which of the seasons of life discussed above sounds most interesting to you?

Which of the seasons of life makes you nervous?

Will You Receive Advice When It Is True?

"You are my friends if you do what I command" would have been a strange-sounding challenge from Jesus to his disciples (John 15:14). This was their rabbi, their leader, their teacher, and the hope of their future. They were not used to thinking of the authority in their lives as a friend. Jesus, however, understood that a part of friendship is giving and receiving advice. Your friends observe you in many different settings. They see the best in you, the worst in you, and the mediocre in you. There are times when your friends possess the perspective in life that you need. Healthy friends, therefore, accept advice from their friends when they are right.

This is an especially difficult part of a marriage friendship. Your love gives you an intense level of influence since you can reach a place in each other's heart that no one else can reach. As a result, your encouragement of one another is more motivating than anyone else in your life. Likewise, any criticism you share with one another has the potential to hurt at a deeper level than anyone else on earth can access.

I (Bill) am still amazed at how hurt I can become when Pam points out something that ought to be corrected in my life. Just recently we were at a Bible study together. I was in a circle with three other men when Pam bolted into the room and corrected something I was saying. In content, she was correct, but the impact of her actions triggered a reaction in me that made me feel like a scolded little boy. I felt stupid, embarrassed, and as if I had just burned my man card in front of my friends. It took me most of three days to recover, even though I would be the first to admit I was overreacting.

I (Pam) am equally amazed at how quickly the thought, *You are so stupid*, rises to the surface any time Bill shares "constructive criticism." I trust Bill more than anyone in the world. I consider him one of the wisest people I know, and yet I want him to share only positive comments with me because even the slightest negative input from him touches a place in my heart that is ridiculously insecure and vulnerable.

For instance, Bill recently approached me and asked, "Pam, can we talk about the way we are managing the database in the office?" Now, I know that Bill is more talented than I am when it comes to technology and systematic organization, but I didn't respond as if I knew that. Internally, it was as if a loudspeaker went off in my heart announcing, "Pam has no idea what she is doing. For years she has been doing it wrong. Bill finally got up enough courage to tell her, so here comes the big evaluation of what a terrible leader Pam is."

Wow, it happened so fast I didn't have time to even slow it down, let alone stop it. Intellectually, I knew I was overreacting, but emotionally, Bill's opinion of me is so important that I couldn't seem to help myself, and I blurted out, "I'm not stupid! You know that, right?"

Despite these quick, insecure responses, we both trust each other as friends so we consistently come back to the conversations to discern the true value in the advice. We know that we sincerely care about each other and want to help each other be our best. We can't remain silent because we care too much. We don't want to hurt one another because we want to free one another to be highly effective. In the end, therefore, we value our friendship enough to incorporate each other's insight into our lives. In addition, when we sense we have reacted or responded negatively to the other, because we are loyal, we will come back and revisit the conversation and most often apologize for any faux pas.

Helping each other learn and grow is unavoidable because you are smarter than your partner in some areas of life. Likewise, your romantic partner is more skilled and knowledgeable in other areas. This is the way of friends. They bring insight, knowledge, and proficiencies into our lives that were missing previously. It is normal, therefore, for friends to share what they know with each other.

Jesus invited his followers into a deeper level of friendship when he said, "I have called you friends, for everything that I learned from my Father I have made known to you" (John 15:15). Jesus would never be content with his superiority. He knew, and his disciples knew, that he was smarter, wiser, stronger, and more talented than they were. He could have shown off and humbled them every time they got together. He could have overwhelmed them with his reasoning, overshadowed them with his talent, and overstated their lack of maturity. Instead, he told them in a humble and respectful manner that he would share with them what he had learned. He wanted his friends to benefit from what he had learned through his relationship with God the Father.

Are You Committed to Open Doors of Opportunity for Each Other?

When we see an opportunity that is good for one of our friends, we tell them. When we find a pursuit in life big enough for others to experience also, we tell our friends about it. When we know of a training conference that is high quality, we invite our friends to join us. We want our friends to know about anything that is helping us be a better person.

If you two are friends, you will be committed to do this same thing for each other. This appears to be a major difficulty for modern couples. Many people seemingly get married based on what they can get from the other person. We don't want our spouses to be too busy because we want to dominate their free time. We don't want our spouses to be too ambitious or have too many interests because we want them to respond to our needs whenever we want our needs met. As a result, we end up stifling the growth of the one we love the most rather than looking for ways to open doors of opportunity that help them develop their full potential.

Consider these admonitions from the apostle Paul:

> Be devoted to one another in love. Honor one another above yourselves (Romans 12:10).

> Therefore encourage one another and build each other up... [A]cknowledge those who work hard among you, who care for you in the Lord and who admonish you. Hold them in the highest regard in love because of their work...Make sure that nobody pays back wrong for wrong, but always strive to do what is good for each other and for everyone else (1 Thessalonians 5:11-15).

When you are in the pre-children stage of life, assisting each other as friends is relatively simple. A commitment to be lifelong friends with your spouse takes on a whole new look once you become a family. When our youngest of three sons was less than a year old, Pam's desire to become a writer kicked into another gear. As her friend, I wanted to do all I could to help her succeed. When she came to me with a request to attend an all-day writer's conference, I had mixed emotions. I believed in her as a writer and I recognized it is a natural passion of hers so I was excited about the possibility of her gaining strategic training and networking. Our youngest was breast-feeding, however, so I was going to have to take extraordinary measures to support her by connecting Pam with our son three times during the conference.

Pam was able to get a ride with a friend to the event, but when it was time for the first feeding, I loaded my three sons into the car, along with the necessary paraphernalia to keep them busy all day, and drove to the conference site. After the first breast-feeding session, I headed to the park to play with the boys. On our way back to the conference, we went through a fast-food restaurant drive-thru so we could take lunch to Pam. After lunch, we went to the beach to play. Of course, sand was in every nook and cranny you can imagine, so I had to clean up the kids, get them back in the car with all their stuff, and head back to the conference for the afternoon feeding. The kids and I then headed home where I made them dinner, bathed them, and eventually got them all in bed.

It was a long day filled with hassles, complicated logistics, and challenges to my attitude. When I thought about getting married, I was blind to the fact that days like this would even occur. When it presented itself, however, I recognized it as an important investment in our friendship. These are the activities you share that are seldom enjoyable at the time but become lingering memories in your lifelong friendship.

HIS Perspective

How do you feel about future goals and ambitions of the woman you love?

How do you think her hopes and dreams for the future will affect you and your hopes and dreams?

Her Perspective

How do you feel about future goals and ambitions of the man you love?

How do you think his hopes and dreams for the future will affect you and your hopes and dreams?

Both: Can you each buy into what the other hopes for your future?

Do You Play Well Together?

A big part of being friends is having fun together. It sounds simple since you probably have a network of friends in your life already. In marriage, it is more of a challenge because there are variations in the way men and women approach friendship. When a woman builds a friendship with other women, they share their hopes, dreams, thoughts, and current experiences in a dynamic flow of ideas. They love to interact and talk about what is happening in their lives. Women rate their friendship high when it is rich with conversation, vibrant with emotions, and characterized by cooperation.

Men, on the other hand, build friendship based on activities. They hunt together, fish together, work on computers together, build things together, make music together, and so on. While they do things side by side, they build camaraderie. Sometimes they share what is on their hearts with one another and sometimes they just share the activity. Men rate a friendship high when it is fun, makes them feel capable, and lowers their stress.

Since men and women approach friendship differently, it's important early in the relationship to agree on a plan for dating and having fun throughout your life.

Are You Going to Keep Dating?

The time you spend dating is not an optional activity in your relationship. It is one of the prime activities that gives you energy for everything else in your life. At this point, you are thinking, *Of course dating is important. We go on dates all the time.* The question you will want to consider is, "Why do the majority of married couples severely limit the time they spend dating each other?" In simplest terms, their responsibilities take precedence over their friendship since the average adult doubles their responsibility every ten years. They don't mean to interrupt their friendship. They just fail to make it a priority. To discover if you have a compatible plan for sustained dating, fill out the checklist below and discuss your answers with your partner.

HIS Perspective

I would like us to have a date
☐ once a week   ☐ every other week   ☐ once a month

I like it better when we
☐ date on the same day of the week each time
☐ discuss what day we go out each time we plan a date

I like our dates best when
☐ they are free or nearly free   ☐ we spend a little money
☐ we spend a lot of money

I like our dates best when
☐ I plan the date   ☐ you plan the date
☐ we take turns planning our dates
☐ we plan our dates together

I like our dates to include
☐ just us   ☐ another couple   ☐ a group

Perspective

I would like us to have a date

☐ once a week   ☐ every other week   ☐ once a month

I like it better when we

☐ date on the same day of the week each time
☐ discuss what day we go out each time we plan a date

I like our dates best when

☐ they are free or nearly free   ☐ we spend a little money
☐ we spend a lot of money

I like our dates best when

☐ I plan the date   ☐ you plan the date
☐ we take turns planning our dates
☐ we plan our dates together

I like our dates to include

☐ just us   ☐ another couple   ☐ a group

Just Plain Fun

Once you decide when you will spend time together, you need to decide what you like to do. You have personal preferences of what you like to do with your free time. You should anticipate differences in your individual preferences because each of you is a unique person with a unique background. You may actually like very different activities when you are in charge of your free time, but to build an effective friendship, there must be some activities you like to engage in together. If there is nothing you like to do together, you may be fascinated with each other now, but it will become irritating or boring later on. If there are a few things you like to do together, you will discover a satisfying mixture of personal and shared activities that create memories and interesting conversations.

On the chart below, mark the activities you like to do on your own (or with your circle of friends) and the ones you like to do together. Feel free to add your own ideas to the chart.

HIS Preferences

CASUAL ACTIVITIES

Activity	On my own	Together
Eat a meal	☐	☐
Watch a movie	☐	☐
Attend a rodeo	☐	☐
Shop	☐	☐
Go to antique stores	☐	☐
Go to concerts	☐	☐
Visit museums	☐	☐
	☐	☐
	☐	☐
	☐	☐
	☐	☐
	☐	☐

ACTIVE PURSUITS

Activity	On my own	Together
Take a walk in the neighborhood	☐	☐
Hike a trail	☐	☐
Canoe or kayak	☐	☐
Boat, jet ski, water ski, or sail	☐	☐
Bicycle	☐	☐
Fly a kite	☐	☐
Walk on the beach or around a lake	☐	☐

	On my own	Together
Dance under the stars	☐	☐
Snowboard, snow ski, or ride an inner tube on the snow	☐	☐
Snowmobile	☐	☐
Ride motorcycles or off-road vehicles	☐	☐
Ride a horse	☐	☐
Ride in a carriage, sleigh, or on a hay ride	☐	☐
Snow sled or toboggan	☐	☐
Inner tube down a river	☐	☐
Bowl	☐	☐
	☐	☐
	☐	☐
	☐	☐
	☐	☐
	☐	☐

STRENUOUS PURSUITS

Activity	On my own	Together
Rock climb	☐	☐
Jump rope or work out	☐	☐
Jog	☐	☐
Work out at an athletic club	☐	☐
Lift weights	☐	☐
Jump on a trampoline	☐	☐
Sky dive	☐	☐
Participate in an aerobics or Pilates class	☐	☐
Snorkel or scuba dive	☐	☐
Wind surf	☐	☐
Boogie board or surf	☐	☐

Run a marathon	☐	☐
	☐	☐
	☐	☐
	☐	☐
	☐	☐

Her Preferences

CASUAL ACTIVITIES

Activity	On my own	Together
Eat a meal	☐	☐
Watch a movie	☐	☐
Attend a rodeo	☐	☐
Shop	☐	☐
Go to antique stores	☐	☐
Go to concerts	☐	☐
Visit museums	☐	☐
	☐	☐
	☐	☐
	☐	☐
	☐	☐
	☐	☐

ACTIVE PURSUITS

Activity	On my own	Together
Take a walk in the neighborhood	☐	☐
Hike a trail	☐	☐
Canoe or kayak	☐	☐
Boat, jet ski, water ski, or sail	☐	☐
Bicycle	☐	☐

Activity	On my own	Together
Fly a kite	☐	☐
Walk on the beach or around a lake	☐	☐
Dance under the stars	☐	☐
Snowboard, snow ski, or ride an inner tube on the snow	☐	☐
Snowmobile	☐	☐
Ride motorcycles or off-road vehicles	☐	☐
Ride a horse	☐	☐
Ride in a carriage, sleigh, or on a hay ride	☐	☐
Snow sled or toboggan	☐	☐
Inner tube down a river	☐	☐
Bowl	☐	☐
	☐	☐
	☐	☐
	☐	☐
	☐	☐
	☐	☐

STRENUOUS PURSUITS

Activity	On my own	Together
Rock climb	☐	☐
Jump rope or work out	☐	☐
Jog	☐	☐
Work out at an athletic club	☐	☐
Lift weights	☐	☐
Jump on a trampoline	☐	☐
Sky dive	☐	☐
Participate in an aerobics or Pilates class	☐	☐
Snorkel or scuba dive	☐	☐

Wind surf	☐	☐
Boogie board or surf	☐	☐
Run a marathon	☐	☐
	☐	☐
	☐	☐
	☐	☐
	☐	☐

Do You Laugh Together?

A good laugh will make you feel better physically and emotionally. Friends who laugh together love to be together because a good, strong laugh is good for you in so many ways.

Laughter improves your *physical health* by:

- Relaxing your entire body and leaving your muscles relaxed for up to forty-five minutes after.

- Boosting your immune system as it decreases stress hormones while increasing immune cells and infection-fighting antibodies.

- Triggering the release of endorphins, which promote a general sense of well-being and temporarily alleviate pain.

- Protecting your heart through increased blood flow. [8]

Laughter improves your *mental health* by:

- Combating emotions that intensify stress since it is nearly impossible to feel anxious, angry, or sad when you're laughing.

- Helping you relax, recharge, and increase your energy level.

- Shifting your perspective away from negative conclusions, which allows you to see situations more realistically. [9]

Laughter is good for your *social health* by:

* Triggering the release of oxytocin, which increases your sense of connection to one another.

* Reminding you not to take yourself so seriously. No matter how hard you try, you will make mistakes. You can either berate yourself or joyfully accept that you are just like the rest of the human race that is striving to find fulfillment and stability in the midst of imperfection.

As a couple, you ought to ask if you are too serious to face life together. Life will be filled with setbacks, surprises, and stress inducing demands. You will face tragedies as well as triumphs. You will experiences success as well as sadness. You will most likely experience pain and progress in equal measure, and you have only so much control over the mixture. Without a healthy habit of laughing, you will put too many expectations on your own behavior, blame each other for problems, and waste the energy you could be using to solve issues by engaging in conflict with each other.

As a check to see if you are ready to face life together, ask yourself the following questions:

Can You Laugh at Yourself?

Our imperfections create plenty of opportunities to be amused at our own behavior. When I (Bill) was a young pastor, I was trying to train our worship team to start the service with high energy. I sensed I wasn't communicating the concept well, so I decided to join the team for a few weeks and show them what I meant. I confidently stepped on the stage in front of the congregation and enthusiastically said, "Welcome to church this morning. Will you please stand and worship me!"

Of course, I meant to say "worship *with* me," but I forgot a very important four-letter word. I was just twenty-nine years old, and I had been at this church only three months, so I think they wondered if I really meant it. I knew I had said something wrong because everyone had a look of shock on their faces. I stopped to think about what I had said and immediately started laughing. The shock on their faces changed to amusement, and they started laughing with me. I attempted to start the service several times, but I snickered every time I tried. We didn't get much done that morning, but it was one of the more memorable services we ever shared together.

Do You Collect Jokes and Funny Stories?

As we were doing research for this book, we came across these two quotes that gave us a good laugh:

- "I never make the same mistake twice. I make it five or six times, you know, just to make sure." [10]
- "The problem with the world is that the intelligent people are full of doubts while the stupid ones are full of confidence." [11]

When we find a humorous joke, story, or quote, we save it in a computer file and email it to each other. If you have trouble laughing as a couple, you are setting yourself up for higher stress than those who regularly amuse themselves.

Are You Able to Respond to Tension-Breaking Moments?

We all experience moments in the midst of difficult situations that unexpectedly break the tension and cause us to break out in laughter, if we let them.

In *Not Another Dating Book*, our good friend Renee Fisher shares several stories from the dating experiences of other young adults. We found a couple of them especially amusing:

> It was my first date with this guy I'd liked forever. He took me to Olive Garden and ordered salad without dressing for us. I looked surprised, and he informed me that "Dressing's really fattening. I don't think you need it."—Shelli, 28

> I met a guy from eHarmony at a park in our neighborhood. He talked about himself the *whole time*. I couldn't get a

single word in edgewise. Finally, after forty-five minutes, he said, "Well, is there anything else you want to know about me?" No, thanks. I'm good.—Michelle, 25 [12]

In both of these situations, these women knew for sure these were not the right men for them because they were creating awkward moments that had no hope of improving.

In contrast, Renee's relationship with her husband, Marc, is a safe haven. She writes, "When Marc asked me out I was flabbergasted. Somebody liked me—finally! I seriously thought he liked my best friend, Amy…He didn't. He was just waiting to ask me out. He said it was after reading my blog that he really fell for me. All that passion and risk he saw me take drew him to me." [13] Renee is one of the most energetic and expressive people we know. She is prone to outbreaks of enthusiasm. Her introverted husband is adept at just smiling, wrapping his arms around her, and saying, "All that passion and all that risk," which gets them both to smiling.

The laughter doesn't fix things that need to be addressed, but it sure does set a great mood for working on it.

Is Our Friendship Healthy?

We know this seems a strange question for those who are considering getting married, but it is vital to a successful lifelong relationship. Marriage is a study in contrasts. Some couples experience an incredible journey together where they support one another, enjoy each other, and figure out life together. We can all think of couples who inspire us to believe in marriage. Other couples manipulate, frustrate, berate, and even abuse each other. Likewise, we all know couples who are so hard on each other we wonder why they ever got married. If you can establish that you, in fact, have a healthy interaction with each other, you can enter marriage with confidence and boldness. If you discover that your relationship is not healthy, you have no business getting married to each other no matter how much you think you are in love. To determine the health of your relationship, be honest with your answers to the strategic questions throughout the following section.

Are we trustworthy friends?

Your first impression is probably, "Of course we are. We wouldn't be together if we weren't." While that may be true, it is also true that "love is blind" and the heart is easily fooled. Trustworthiness comes down to habits. Anyone can appear trustworthy for a short period of time, but habits will eventually rule the day and determine the atmosphere of your relationship. Healthy habits demonstrate quality character development and dedication to personal growth. Unhealthy habits point to a self-centered, immature approach to life that will be insufficient to handle the realities of marriage.

To help you determine how healthy your partner's habits are, fill out the trustworthiness scale below. For each question, rate your partner from 0 to 5: 0 means you wouldn't recommend this behavior to anyone; 3 means their approach is adequate; 5 means you consider your partner to be a role model everyone ought to emulate. To help you formulate your response, read the supporting questions listed below the chart.

HIS Perspective

Trustworthiness Scale	How I rate my partner	Score
Is my partner the same person online and in real life?	0 1 2 3 4 5	
Does my partner have healthy work relationships?	0 1 2 3 4 5	
Does my partner have a healthy social and family circle?	0 1 2 3 4 5	
How healthy is my partner's financial status?	0 1 2 3 4 5	
How well does my partner handle responsibility?	0 1 2 3 4 5	
How is my partner's personal hygiene?	0 1 2 3 4 5	
	Total:	

Perspective

Trustworthiness Scale	How I rate my partner	Score
Is my partner the same person online and in real life?	0 1 2 3 4 5	
Does my partner have healthy work relationships?	0 1 2 3 4 5	
Does my partner have a healthy social and family circle?	0 1 2 3 4 5	
How healthy is my partner's financial status?	0 1 2 3 4 5	
How well does my partner handle responsibility?	0 1 2 3 4 5	
How is my partner's personal hygiene?	0 1 2 3 4 5	
	Total:	

This is a personal survey not a scientific test, but the score will reveal a lot about your relationship. If the total is under 18, you should honestly ask if this is the right person for you. A score of 24 or higher indicates confidence in your dating partner as a trustworthy person in your life.

Is my love interest the same person online and in real life?

- What is being written on their Facebook, Twitter, or other social media accounts? Social media encourages a stream of consciousness that often removes filters people exercise when they are trying to impress you. Is your partner as committed to you online as you are being told face-to-face?

- Who are your romantic partner's online friends and what kind of conversations are they having? Do you notice your partner having conversations that ought to be happening with you?

- Is the one you love recognized in a positive way on his or her workplace website?

- Is your date or romantic partner on any watch lists? You can check to see if they are a sex offender at www.sexualof fenders.com. If you discover that a watch list is involved, is there a reasonable, credible explanation? Are they defensive about you asking or can you talk calmly and honestly about what it means?

Does my romantic partner have healthy work relationships?

- Do you know anyone from the company where they work? What do these people say about the one you love?

- Do you know their employment history and highlights?

- Are you welcome at your dating partner's workplace? If not, is there a reasonable and credible explanation?

Does the one I love have a healthy social and family circle?

- Are they close to their family, and have you met any family members?

- Who are their friends, and are you comfortable with them?

- Where do they spend their off-work time?

- Do they seem to have any friends they do not want you to meet?

How healthy is my dating partner's financial status?

- Are they living within their means or are they stressed by debt?

- Have school loans been repaid? If not, is there a realistic plan in place to pay them off?

- Do they use credit more than you feel comfortable with?

How well does my dating partner handle responsibility?

- Do they work? And how hard?
- Do they abuse or frequently use alcohol, drugs, or tobacco?
- Do they take care of their house (or apartment), car, or yard in a way you are comfortable with?

How is my dating partner's personal hygiene?

- Do they take care of their body in a reasonable way?
- Do they have reasonably healthy eating habits?

Curious or Suspicious?

As you think through the health of your potential life partner's habits, it is important you take a look at yourself also. The point here is to become curious enough about your potential life partner to determine if you can live with the collection of habits that characterize his or her life. It is all too easy to become suspicious rather than curious. You look through their email for inappropriate conversations. You scan social media with a critical eye looking for a lack of character. You interrogate acquaintances at work to make sure nothing inappropriate is going on. Suspicion comes from a desire to control the other person so you feel safe. Curiosity comes from a sincere desire to see the relationship truthfully so you can make an informed, confident decision.

You can tell if you have a healthy curiosity because you aren't afraid of what you will find. If you are suspicious, you are not ready to get married! Where do you rate yourself on a scale from *curious* to *suspicious*?

How do you feel about your answer?

DATE *to* DISCOVER

Each of you make a list of shared activities you both might be able to enjoy for a lifetime—travel, food tasting, sports, dancing, art, home improvement. Each select a date off the other person's list you are willing to try to see if it's a shared activity you might want to keep in your future. Set a date within the next two weeks to try these two activities. After both dates, debrief and rate the activity 1 to 5, with 5 being the top score. (You can keep trying things with this system if you'd like all through your dating, engagement, and on into marriage!)

A Little Adam *&* Eve Humor

One day, after being thrust out of the garden, Adam and Abel are walking past the Garden of Eden.

Abel: "So, Dad, you and Mom used to live in there, huh?"

Adam: "Yes, son, it was lovely."

Abel: "Why did you leave?"

Adam: "Your mother ate us out of house and home."

Are We Compatible?

Delight in the Differences

> *Me got him.*
> *He got me.*
> *We got us.*
> *You got that?*[1]

Who doesn't love a buffet? A smorgasbord offers a plethora of foods and a wide variety of tastes sure to please the palate. While a buffet carries many tantalizing flavors, you may have rejected, walked past, or been afraid to try some of the culinary treats presented for your pleasure. As you combine your life with someone you think you love, it could feel like taking a Mexican fiesta party buffet and merging it with a French fine-dining experience or you might be trying to pair a vegan menu with a carnivorous barbeque. The differences can widen your life and broaden your horizons. If, however, differences are neither accepted nor appreciated, they become the dynamite that blows the relationship apart.

Tools to Maximize Our Differences

Differences can either be appreciated or drive people apart. When you can see the value of the different ways God wired people, it is easier to get along with them. The more tools you have in your toolbox, the easier it will be to see how to value the different ways God created people, including the one you love. You will also gain an appreciation for how to use those differences to add strength to your relationship. Some relational tools are intended to simply keep you motivated, which sounds exciting at first. These are the power tools of life. When you turn them on, power surges through your heart, empowering you to face opportunities that come your way. They are necessary because the demands of life require a lot of energy.

As a single individual, you can organize life around your natural motivation, which minimizes stress as you raise your energy level. Getting married makes this more difficult because you are most likely attracted to someone with a different motivational style. It is further complicated by the tendency to assume others are motivated the same way we are. One of the great challenges, therefore, of being in a relationship is learning to accept and appreciate each other's motivational makeup.

The following are some natural motivational tools, which we'll look at more closely in the discussion that follows:

Pace of life
Temperament style
Conflict-resolution style
Love language
Birth order
Relax-and-recharge style
Spiritual gift
Parenting styles

What's Your Pace?

Each of us has a God-given pace in life. We can operate at this pace for extended periods of time because it is what we were designed for. Bicycles have gears so cyclists can stay at their pace. When their feet are spinning faster than their pace, they grow fatigued. Similarly, when their feet are going slower than their natural pace, they also become fatigued. The gears allow them to find the right pace regardless of the terrain.

The importance of finding your pace is referred to in 1 Corinthians

9:24. "Do you not know that in a race all the runners run, but only one gets the prize? Run in such a way as to get the prize." Paul borrows a picture from the Olympic Games to challenge our approach to life. A participant in a 100-yard dash will sprint to the finish while a marathoner will run at a consistent, but not frenetic, pace. To win, they need to run their race at their pace.

It will be less stressful if each person in your family knows his or her pace or the speed at which they function best. In Bill's book, *The 10 Best Decisions a Man Can Make* (and the DVD series that goes with it),[2] he shares an easy-to-use way to identify and evaluate your pace by using five vehicles that illustrate the characteristics for the speed at which each of us can live: Muscle Car, Sports Car, Semi, Mail Truck, and Tractor. Once you've read the descriptions for each vehicle, take time to discuss on a date or with friends over coffee which vehicle best represents your personal pace. It makes for some interesting conversation! It also leads to greater understanding and fewer arguments as you get to know those you love better.

Muscle Car

Muscle cars have big engines and are designed to go in a straight line with an abundance of pull and dramatic speed. Muscle-car people like to go fast and focus forward, charging hard toward goals. They often make quick decisions and pursue big opportunities. A biblical example is the apostle Paul who, after his dramatic conversion, quickly turned into a prolific church planter.

Sports Car

Some of you move more like sports cars. These vehicles are fun, agile, and quick. They prefer roads that have lots of turns and quick transitions. Sports-car people live for the surprise around the next corner. They tend to be spontaneous in decision-making and can change directions quickly to take advantage of what they see as a great opportunity. A biblical example is Philip, who was on his way to one city when God sent him in a completely different direction so someone could hear about the love of God (Acts 8:26-40).

Semi

Some people operate more like a semitruck. These people start and stop slowly because they prefer to plan out life. They maintain a steady and even pace and often carry a great amount of faithful, day-in-and-day-out responsibility. They do not like quick change because they require time to navigate course corrections. A biblical example is Martha, who handled most of the hospitality for a house full of Jesus' followers.

Mail Truck

Mail-truck people have a sign on their backs, "Makes Frequent Stops." They are intensely interested in others and are peaceful even if life is consistently interrupted by conversations, projects, and helping people. Life has a route, but their pace is slower because they are constantly checking on the well-being of people in their world. A biblical example is Barnabas, who set aside his agenda to take on John Mark as a mentoring project until John Mark was mature and ready to lead again (Acts 15:36-39).

Tractor

Tractors are incredibly useful, but they move slowly. People who fit this category dig in their heels if pushed to accomplish tasks too fast. These folks also do not enjoy sharp turns and tend to work at a slower, even pace, even if the schedule suggests they should speed up to make a deadline. A biblical example might be Ruth, who daily went to the grain fields to glean (a slow, steady task) in order to provide for her and her mother-in-law (Ruth 2:1-3).

In our family, I (Pam) am a speedy, spontaneous sports car. Bill is a faithful, people-oriented mail truck. We have one son who is like me, one who is a muscle car, and another who is a semi. Before I recognized that each person's pace is a God-given gift for that person to live out their unique calling, I used to be frustrated that my "semi" slowed down our family's ability to get out the door. And Bill, whose natural pace as a mail truck is slower than mine, could get frustrated with me, feeling pulled away from people and dragged through life at a pace where deep, meaningful conversations were harder to accomplish. Because two of us are sports cars, the others in the family have learned to trust our instincts for seizing opportunities. Their lives have become more fun and interesting because of our "Let's try this *now!*" attitude. And when a task hits our family, such as a broken washing machine, my engineer semi is just the man for the job. On family vacations, we decide what the family pace will be before we arrive to minimize the battle of emotional expectations. As our sons have married, knowing the life pace of my daughters-in-law helps avoid misunderstandings or hurt feelings.

 Love Chat

- Which of the five vehicles best represents the pace at which you like to live?
- What do you believe the person you love would say is his or her pace?
- What is a positive impact of their pace?
- What frustrations do you have with your partner's pace?
- What pace do you believe is best for you as a couple when you need to work or decide together?

Temperament Style

Your temperament determines the way you process the information of life. You discover your temperament by asking two strategic questions: "Am I more extroverted or introverted?" and "Am I more people-oriented or task-oriented?"

Introverts look at life from the inside out. They ask questions such as, "Do I feel emotionally connected to you?" "Does this career make me feel fulfilled?" "Do I feel close to God?" Introverts think before they speak. Sometimes they think long and hard.

Extroverts look at life from the outside in. They ask, "Am I spending enough time at work to climb the ladder?" "Am I spending enough time on my priorities?" "Am I doing the things that will build my relationships?" Extroverts tend to share whatever comes across their mind, so don't panic, they are just thinking out loud!

Do you look at life from the outside in (extrovert) or from the inside out (introvert)?

Task-oriented individuals are very good at getting things done. Given the opportunity to spend time with people or finish a task, they will work on the task at hand with the thought, *Everyone will be better when we get done with this.* People-oriented individuals are very good at spending time with others. They can get things done, but they are easily distracted when others walk by because they sincerely want to know what is going on with these people. They firmly believe that everything will get done when everyone is getting along.

 Love Chat

- Are you more introverted or extroverted?

- Is the one you love more introverted or extroverted?

- Are you more task-oriented or people-oriented?

- Is the one you love more people-oriented or more task-oriented?

- How do you feel about how the one you love is wired?

- How is your life enhanced by the way God has wired him or her?

- Are there any potential pitfalls you will need to navigate because of your differences in these areas? If so, how do you plan to handle this?

What's Your Motivation?

Combining the answers to the two strategic questions ("Am I more extroverted or introverted?" and "Am I more people-oriented or task-oriented?") provides four distinct temperament and motivational types as seen in the chart on the next page.

Lover #1
Knight in
Shining Armor /
Queen of Hearts

- Extroverted
- Task-Oriented
- Likes control of decisions
- Likes people to cooperate
  with their plan
- Adventurous
- Usually in charge

Motivated by Authority

Lover #2
Hopeless
Romantic

- Extroverted
- People-Oriented
- Spontaneous
- Likes new adventures
- Center of attention
- Fun (Does not like boring)
- Likes personal touches

Motivated by Attention

Lover #4
True Blue
Lover

- Introverted
- Task-Oriented
- Likes the predictable
- Likes scheduled activities
- Likes routine
- Believes everyone should
  do what they say

Motivated by Accuracy

Lover #3
Wind Beneath
My Wings

- Introverted
- People-Oriented
- Relaxed
- Easy going
- Likes time to talk
- Likes low stress
- Takes life as it comes

Motivated by Admiration

These temperaments are often referred to as choleric, sanguine, phlegmatic, and melancholy, and a number of variations have been developed over the years. Since this is a book on love, we will refer to them as types of lovers:

- Knight in Shining Armor or Queen of Hearts (Choleric)
- Hopeless Romantic (Sanguine)
- Wind Beneath My Wings (Phlegmatic)
- True-Blue Lover (Melancholy)

An appendix to this book provides references to several resources that can help you determine your temperament and motivational style. We encourage you to consult the many resources listed and have the one you love take the temperament quizzes to discern his or her personality type.

When taking a temperament profile as an adult, try to think back to what you were like as a child of seven or eight. Often as adults we have learned to mask our true self in order to please other people. Or, more positively, we have gained the skills to strengthen our perceived weaknesses with a goal of becoming more like Jesus. (Jesus would, of course, have all the strengths of all the motivation styles and none of the weaknesses!) For each personality temperament, we have given a key word to capture the essence of that motivational outlook.

Knight in Shining Armor or Queen of Hearts (Powerful). These are extroverted, task-oriented decision makers and natural leaders. Bob Phillips labels them *drivers* and the DISC test uses the word *dominant*. Their primary shortcomings are a lack of empathy and a bulldozer mentality. They are so focused on the task at hand, they can sometimes run over people to get it done. They are like *lions* in that they are primarily motivated by exercising authority. Fun to them is anything they decide on. The best way to motivate a Knight or Queen is to give him or her choices. This powerful personality loves to be the leader or boss. Without these personalities, the world might just stop because they are the driving force behind most great goals and dreams. Other people may dream great dreams, but cholerics wake up and make them happen. They are natural leaders so John Trent and Gary Smalley refer to these as lions as they like having control over their world in a "king of the jungle" decision maker type way.

Hopeless Romantic (Popular). The other extrovert is the people-oriented sanguine. These people are like *otters* because they love to have fun. Phillips calls them *expressive*, the DISC, *inspirational*. They are creative, spontaneous, and have super people skills. Their primary weakness is a lack of perseverance (if it isn't fun, why stay at it?). They love a party, so they can seem shallow and flippant to some of the other personalities. They are primarily motivated by people and praise. All they want is a little attention—okay, a lot of attention—and they will do anything to get it. If you want to motivate sanguines, hook a task to a person or make it a party, and they are there for you! Without these popular personalities, many of us would have fewer friends. The popular personalities make the world a tolerable, happy place to dwell.

Since I (Pam) am primarily a Hopeless Romantic, I can create ideas in bucketfuls, and I think all of them are brilliant just because I came up with them. I want to set sail with a host of ideas. Bill is my rudder in life, helping me to sort through the ideas, choose the best ones, and make them rise to the level of excellence. Without him, my impatience would cause me to make many mistakes—possibly a few tragic ones.

Wind Beneath My Wings (Peaceful). The phlegmatic is an introverted, amiable, steady, no-frills, peace-at-all costs, likeable guy or gal. Phillips labels these as *amiable*; the DISC says they are *steady*. They are like *retrievers* with their peaceful personality. Everyone gets along with them because their goal in life is not to rock the boat. Everyone likes the retriever unless you want something done, you need a decision out of them, or you are in a hurry. Then they can drive you crazy!

I (Pam) am married to a man whose primary temperate is peaceful. All that a peaceful personality needs in life is to be admired and appreciated. I know I could not do what I do as a leader, traveling speaker, and writer if Bill weren't in my life. He really is the wind beneath my wings. Even while writing this book, I told him, "Honey, I need you. You are my inspiration," and I meant it. People just function better with a little TLC, and the peaceful personalities can give emotional support well.

The theme song of the peaceful personality would be Otis Redding's "Respect," made famous by Aretha Franklin. All they want is a little respect. When you show appreciation and respect to these people, they will do almost anything for you. They might take a while, but they will get it done. Most of us just couldn't get along without these natural mediators.

True-Blue Lover (Processor). This melancholy personality is introverted and task-oriented. Most great artists and musicians have this motivation style. They are creative and they want things done right. They have the patience to do things with excellence. They actually enjoy the process and predictability of life. Their perfectionism or tenacious hold on maintaining the process can drive other people, primarily the sanguine, crazy. The sanguine's response to a melancholy will always be "Lighten up!" But they can't lighten up. The world is seen in detail and is in desperate need of fixing to these folks. They can become negative and depressed because they see the glass half-empty, and they notice all the little undone things in the world.

They are *beavers* because they are hardworking and get the job done. The DISC test calls them *cautious*, and Bob Phillips labels them as *analytical.* They are always thinking, always processing.

So if you are married to a True-Blue Lover, make very few promises and keep the ones you make, or you will lose credibility. They are motivated by accuracy, so if you say you are going to be home at 6:00 p.m., you'd better do it. If you come in at 6:20, you weren't late—you lied. The processor personality takes most things literally. Without them, the world would be filled with so many more mistakes. Imagine the processors as those who set all the synchronized traffic lights. Chaos would happen without them!

What's Your Conflict-Resolution Style?

If you step into the boxing arena, you will hear terms such as *southpaw, outside fighter,* or *palooka* to describe boxing styles. In the same way, we each have a way we react when issues crop up in relationships. Stress and conflict bring out different responses in different people, and you do well to know how your future mate tends to solve problems. Once you know his or her bent, you can work with it to create a pattern that is workable for the two of you to get to resolution.

How you manage conflict is a primary predictor of whether your marriage will make it the distance. For example, if one of you is always in attack mode and the other just stuffs down his or her feelings, one day you might come home to an empty house or to a locked front door with your earthly belongings set ablaze on the front drive.

The following are some samples of conflict-resolution styles.

Negotiators

These couples like to brainstorm. They are always looking for new ways to solve problems. They like to explore options, ask other people for their opinions, and research books and magazines about their situation. Discovering different ways to approach a problem gives them a sense of security. When they have solutions to choose from, they feel confident they can choose the best option available. These people resolve problems methodically, and they often put discussions on hold until they can gather more information.

Debaters

These couples are loud and love to argue. From the outside, they look contentious and out of control. People are amazed that they even like each other. They may argue passionately, but they know how to make up passionately! Often these are intellectuals who enjoy the sparring of wits, or they are the down-to-earth type who love the feeling of sparks flying.

Peacekeepers

These couples have figured out how to agree to disagree. They don't argue over much, but they also don't ignore issues. They easily defer to each other and appear to everyone else to be naturally happy. They are by nature "go with the flow" types, so even when they disagree with each other, they have a "things will work themselves out" attitude. These folks sometimes allow real issues to go dormant for years until growing stress or discontent force them to face the problem. Sometimes just one is a true peacekeeper, so he or she will just go along with the more opinionated party.

Drama Team

These folks might argue with flamboyance, but they make up with equal flair! These couples are very intense about life and forgiveness. They want everything on the table. They want to know the details and to talk through everything. They have aggressively accepted that life is imperfect, and they expect this from each other. They consistently forgive each other and repent for their mistakes in a pursuit of excellence. They have a "we have survived so far so we can survive this too" attitude. Love feels more real and authentic if emotions are shared with some intensity and drama. Neither seems deterred from love or the relationship even if the disagreements include raised voices or intense body movements and expressions.

Survivors

These couples may not have great skills, but they always end up together. They may have past emotional baggage, or one of the partners may be overwhelmed by the demands of life. They probably approach their conflicts in different ways, and one of the spouses may work harder than the other at resolutions. They stay married by their sheer determination to stay married. They have frequent periods when they do not enjoy their relationship, but they keep finding ways to rediscover their love.

Servants

These couples identify who is most affected by the stress of their lives, and the other spouse commits to serve. During the struggle, expectations are low and sacrifices are high. This tends to be our conflict-resolution style. When we are in an argument, neither of us is very good at staying angry. We both make moves toward each other and toward serving or sacrificing to create a plan for connection. When there is any disagreement or tension, we know the other person is likely praying and asking God for a solution. We both apologize readily. We don't hold errors against each other but make "us" and unity the priority. Sometimes solutions to the issues take weeks, even months to discern, but we both still make every effort to move toward each other.

 Love Chat

Which conflict-resolution style best describes you? Which best describes the one you love?

- Negotiator
- Debater
- Peacekeeper
- Drama team
- Survivor
- Servant

Speak the Right Love Language

We highly recommend Gary Chapman's *The Five Love Languages*. All the expressions of love listed below can be effective, but each of us has a favorite way to receive love from our spouse.

My (Pam's) primary love language is *acts of service*. When Bill makes time to bail me out, helps me work out a technology bug, or gives me directions over the phone when I get lost, he speaks volumes of love to me. My secondary love language is *words of affirmation*, but those words must be sincere for me to really feel wowed. Bill prefers *quality time*, so sharing meals each day is a priority to him. He also loves when I set aside time to listen and be a sounding board so he can verbally process issues he is seeking to gain clarity on. If I buy him a gift, he values it, but what he really wanted was for me to sit down and listen to his heart. Time given is more effective. If Bill refused to help me succeed as a writer and speaker, or blocked the path to my hopes and dreams, but bought me a diamond necklace, I might be so upset that I'd sell the necklace to fund an assistant.

Listen to your love's heartbeat! How does he or she best receive love? And as you look toward a lifelong commitment, are you able to give love this way for a lifetime?

 *Love Chat*

If you had to choose, which would be your favorite way for your mate to express his or her love toward you?

- *Words of affirmation* (encouraging words, words that build you up)
- *Physical touch* (pat on the back, holding hands, hugs, and more)
- *Quality time* (making the effort to enjoy relaxed time with meaningful connections)
- *Acts of service* (helping the one you love succeed by doing tasks with and for them)
- *Gifts* (small tokens of affection, symbolic gifts, or costly presents all count)

Birth Order

Your placement in the family you grew up in influenced who you are today. In *The Birth Order Book*, Kevin Leman offers a sample quiz to help the reader get a quick grasp of the influence of birth order:

> Which of the following sets of personality traits fits you the best? You don't have to meet all the criteria in a certain list of traits. Just pick the list that has the most items that seem to describe you and your way of operating in life.
>
> A. perfectionist, reliable, conscientious, a list maker, well organized, hard driving, a natural leader, critical, serious, scholarly, logical, doesn't like surprises, a techie
>
> B. mediator, compromising, diplomatic, avoids conflict, independent, loyal to peers, has many friends, a maverick, secretive, used to not having attention
>
> C. manipulative, charming, blames others, attention seeker, tenacious, people person, natural salesperson, precocious, engaging, affectionate, loves surprises
>
> D. little adult by age seven, very thorough, deliberate, high achiever, self-motivated, fearful, cautious, voracious reader, black-and-white thinker, talks in extremes, can't bear to fail, has very high expectations for self, more comfortable with people who are older or younger [3]

You have probably figured out that A, B, and C listed traits in order from the oldest to the youngest in the family. If you picked list A, it's a good bet you are the firstborn in your family. If you chose list B, chances are you are a middle child. If list C seemed to best describe who you are, it's likely you are the baby in the family. But what about list D? It describes the only child.

Two middle children have the best odds at long-term love because they are trained to negotiate and compromise as part of the family dynamic. Two firstborns need lots of relational training because they will both want to be in charge. Two babies will have a fun time, but they might not get all their responsibilities accomplished.

I (Pam) need to know that Bill, as the baby of his family, often got overlooked, and his voice and opinions were not taken seriously. I need to tune in and seek to give validity to his views. Bill needs to know that as a firstborn, I am used to being in charge—of something—so as a wise leader of a firstborn wife, he will delegate pieces of our life to me to oversee and I will be happier.

 *Love Chat*

- My placement in the family is:
- The one I love's place in the family is:
- How does your placement in your family of origin affect the way you relate to people?
- How does it affect the way you relate to the one you love?

Relax-and-Recharge Style

If you do marry, you might have very different views about what is relaxing on a honeymoon, a vacation, or a day off. What renews, revives, and rejuvenates you and the person you love? Will you be able to not just work together but enjoy playing together? Here are some relax-and-recharge styles that may accurately describe you and your future mate:

Busy bee: Even on vacation this person has a to-do list. He or she comes into a vacation or day off with a schedule and plan.

Social butterfly: These people believe vacations are all about relationship, so driving two days each way on a five-day trip is just fine if they can see people who are important to them.

Waiting walking stick: These people like to sit still on vacation or a day off. Give them a hammock and a book, and they are happy.

Active ant: These people enjoy activities and athletics on their days off. You'll find them jet skiing, kayaking, snowboarding, hiking, and the like.

Luggage ladybug: These people prefer guided tours, group outings, and professionals in charge of their free time.

If you talk through your downtime, keeping your style in mind, less of free time will be used for arguments and more of it used for fun activities.

The Gender Gap

In addition to relaxing styles, gender influences the way we reduce stress. In *Men Are Like Waffles—Women Are Like Spaghetti*, we explain that women process stress by talking their way through it. If I (Pam) am stressed, my mom knows it, my sister knows it, my best friend knows it, my prayer partner knows it—the clerk at the grocery store will know it! However, if Bill is stressed, he will want to go to one of his favorite "easy boxes" to rest and recharge. It's like a battery in a battery recharger. God helped us women out so we can recognize these favorite boxes of men, as most are shaped like boxes—the TV screen, the garage, the football field, basketball court, and baseball diamond—all boxes. The pool table, computer, and even the refrigerator are box shaped as well. And once you are married, the bed (or sex box) will be a favorite box for your husband to go to when life is stressful. It's like the "free square" on a bingo card, and husbands can get there from every other square!

 *Love Chat*

- How does the difference between genders impact you and your dating relationship when you are each stressed?
- What can you do that will help lower the stress of the one you love?
- What activities most renew, rejuvenate, and revive you?
- What relaxing style do you have? What style does the one you love have?

Because life is stressful, this has become a vital area to negotiate a plan of action for life and love. So take time and each explain to the other what raises stress in your life and what lowers it. What can you do to help each other when life ramps up and stress is rising?

Unwrap the Gift

I (Pam) fell in love with Bill because he was so compassionate. However, I soon found that his compassion applied to all of humankind! People who are in distress seek out Bill because he is a gifted people helper. If we are walking down a crowded city street and a homeless person sees us approach, he or she will *always* talk to Bill and ask for help. If Bill is with a group of men and someone's car has a flat or they've locked their keys in the car, that person will *always* ask Bill for help.

This is so predictable, it has become comical. Once when leaving for an anniversary vacation in Hawaii, I bought Bill a T-shirt that read "Witness Protection Program: You don't know me!" It still didn't help. Even then people in need approached him. He turned to me and asked, "What is it with me? Why do I always look like the one who can solve a person's problem?" I smiled and said, "Might be the Superman cape sticking out from under your shirt."

Then it hit me. That had been my nickname for Bill nearly all our married life: Superman. I had seen that quality in him when I was a twenty-year-old and I adored it. At times now when we are on a family trip and his cell phone rings with a crisis on the other end, I get frustrated or even angry. I think to myself, *Why does the whole world need him? Can't their problems wait just one day while we spend time together?*

Over the years, we had to learn to make compromises. I learned that having to share Bill with others is a small price to pay to be married to a man with his amazing heart and character. He learned to set up boundaries and protect days off, holidays, and vacations. He decided to meet people only at the office so our home could be a place of rest and family connection.

We should make room for one another's gifts instead of being frustrated by them. For example, a couple can become frustrated if the wife has the gift of hospitality and the husband doesn't like having lots of people around or doesn't want people to mess with his stuff. Can you see how a situation like this might cause some anxiety even though it involves your area of strength?

These various gifts are God-given and enhance your life in a powerful way. They can also disrupt your life if they run unchecked. A couple can come to a place of agreement by being aware of each other's gifts and making allowances for them. Consider a couple who is asked to team teach. If he has the gift of teaching but she has the gift of helps, he could teach and she could handle hospitality, provide resources, and make phone calls. While staying in the background, she can be available for individual discussions to help people apply the material to their lives. This gives them both the opportunity to work in their comfort range.

The social butterfly married to "the king of the castle" type might compromise and create a home that is guest-friendly but includes a private space that is off-limits to company. That way, he can retreat if the company chaos becomes too much for him.

Talk with your mate about the list of gifts below. This is not an exhaustive list but rather a place to begin the dialogue. Discuss how you can make room for each other's gifts and find creative solutions for any differences.

- Administration: directing projects (Romans 12:8; 1 Corinthians 12:5,28)

- Craftsmanship and artistry: using your hands to create or build so that others are pointed toward God (Exodus 30:22-25; 2 Chronicles 34:9-13; Acts 16:14; 18:3)

- Evangelism: communicating spiritual truth to lead someone to a personal relationship with God (Acts 5:42; Romans 10:15; Ephesians 4:11; 2 Timothy 4:5)

- Exhortation: encouraging people and walking alongside them to bring out the best in them (Romans 12:8; 1 Corinthians 2:1-2; 2 Corinthians 9:2)

- Giving: providing faithful stewardship and sharing with others (Mark 12:41-44; Luke 18:12; Romans 12:8; 2 Corinthians 8:1-7)

- Helps and serving: caring for others by working behind the scenes (Mark 2:3-4; Luke 22:22-27; Romans 16:1-2; 12:7; 1 Corinthians 12:28; 1 Timothy 6:2; 1 Peter 4:9-10)

- Hospitality: using the home or other resources to make people feel included and welcomed (Acts 16:15; 21:16-17; Romans 12:9-13; 16:23)

- Intercession: devoting time and energy to pray (Acts 12:1-17; 16:25-31; Colossians 4:12; 1 Timothy 2:1-8)

- Knowledge: sharing information that helps people live in a productive, healthy manner (Romans 15:14; 1 Corinthians 12:8; 13:8)

- Leadership: directing people (1 Timothy 5:17)

- Mercy: showing compassion and acting to meet needs (Luke 10:33-35; Acts 9:36; 16:33-34; Romans 12:8)

- Music: singing or playing instruments to turn hearts toward God (1 Samuel 16:16; 1 Chronicles 16:41-42; 2 Chronicles 5:12-13)

- Prophecy: publicly proclaiming truth (Ezra 6:1; Isaiah 14:28; 20:45; 25:1; 1 Corinthians 12:10; 13:2; 14:1)

- Teaching: explaining concepts to others and helping them apply them (Romans 12:7; 1 Corinthians 12:28; Ephesians 4:11; 1 Timothy 3:2)

- Wisdom: applying knowledge with discretion and insight (2 Chronicles 1:11-12; Proverbs 1:2; 2:10)

- Writing: communicating information to help others grow in faith, develop life skills, or turn toward God (Psalm 45:1; Acts 15:19-20; Philippians 3:1; 1 Timothy 3:14-15)

You might decide to take an online gifts test. A simple one we have used is sponsored by Rock Church in San Diego (www.sdrock.com/giftstest/).

 *Love Chat*

- What is your spiritual gift(s)?
- What are the gifts of the one you love?
- Are these gifts compatible if you both exercise them?
- How can you best support each other as you seek to live out your God-given giftedness?

Parenting Style

Even if you do not have children, you do have views about how kids should be raised. You have a parenting style that will guide your actions with your children. The way you parent is a combination of what you saw modeled by your parents and what you have decided to apply on your own. Good parenting is not automatic. You can learn to become a better parent, or you can deteriorate in your parenting skills. The most effective parenting is proactive but requires a lot of energy and focus. You can begin to be a proactive parent by identifying your starting point and creating a plan for growth. Which of these styles best describes you?

- *Permissive*: These parents border on apathy or neglect. They are too busy, too broken, or too self-absorbed to care.
- *Popular*: These parents are so concerned about maintaining a friendship with their child that they won't risk the friendship by enforcing rules, boundaries, or discipline.
- *Paranoid*: These parents worry about everything and make decisions based upon fear.
- *Prescriptive*: These parents wait until issues become problems before they act.
- *Proactive*: These parents prayerfully set goals, make plans, and discuss parenting choices ahead of time to guide and lead a child forward.

We encourage you to read a parenting book even before you are married and well before you have children. Our book *The 10 Best Decisions a Parent Can Make* gives an overview on children from cradle through college. If you are blending families, we recommend you go to www.smartstepfamilies.com and select resources to read together, or pick up Debbie and Ray Alsdorf's *Beyond the Brady Bunch: Hope and Help for Blended Families*.

Blended or starting out fresh, this is such a vital topic that no one should marry until you have discussed some core issues on family life. Choose a parenting book. Read and discuss your views and opinions. To get you started, take time for a quick love chat on how you were parented and what you will keep and what you will replace when you have your own kids.

♥ Love Chat ♥

- How many children do you want?
- Is this different than the number the one you love wants?
- How will you handle deciding on how many children you will have?
- What did your parents do right?
- What would you do differently?
- What style of parenting best fits you?
- How close is this to the style of the one you love and his or her approach to parenting?
- What do you think is the most critical key to raising children who grow up to be strong citizens, strong Christians, and strong people who have a strong love life and marriage?

So What Now?

Now that we know all these things about ourselves, what do we do with the information? We have some choices. We can use it against each other, bringing it up in arguments or manipulating to gain an advantage. Or we can use it to excuse our own unhealthy behaviors. Neither of these do we recommend, obviously, because God wants us to grow in grace and mature in areas of weakness.

A much more useful approach is to discover each other's strengths and uniqueness. These very qualities caused you to fall in love with each other, so if you stay aware of these traits, you can use them to strengthen your relationship.

Bill often tells others he is living a much larger life because he is married to me. He is so easygoing that he would not naturally choose the visionary, idealistic path. He is so people-oriented that he would stop all along the way with a goal of meeting every person he encountered.

I am so visionary and idealistic that I can forget to count the costs of decisions ahead of time. I am prone to thinking I can just handle those things as they come along. Because I am so extroverted, I can be tempted to live a shallow life. Because I am married to Bill, I have learned to use my gifts of writing and speaking to share all the wonderful, deep, practical, people-helping information Bill has created. God has formed us into an effective team. Bill creates materials that are proven to help people, and I package and present them. I envision what can be. Bill ensures our plans are thought through, and then I push them forward by my faith.

The Gift of Acceptance

In order to utilize these motivational tools, you must accept each other. Accepting and celebrating your differences allows each of you to use these traits and affirm each other as a unique creation of God. When I graduated from college, Bill gathered my friends and threw a "This Is Your Life" party. Several of the blondes acted out different stages of my life. I have never laughed so hard as I watched them make a melodrama from all my habits and idiosyncrasies.

When Bill was celebrating his ten-year anniversary as senior pastor, I gathered some friends to celebrate. They created a humorous and poignant drama of all the things Bill could have been (coach, counselor, draftsman, or doctor) if he hadn't followed the call to pastoral ministry and how he was using all those skills in his ministry to people. He felt valued and appreciated.

Look for a way to observe your romantic partner and celebrate him or her. What trait can you encourage and appreciate? Romance is nothing more than seeing the masterpiece God has given you in the one you love and taking the time to applaud him or her. Box up your admiration, tie it with a bow, and give it with your sincere verbal praise.

Now it's your turn. Open your relational toolbox and identify the resources you can use to build your relationship. Share the answers to your motivational sheets below and try to identify which area brings most strength to your love and which area will more likely be a source of contention. Try to find a mentor couple who can give you insight in the area of weakness so your love is shored up. If most areas are a potential problem, it's time to discuss with a mentor, counselor, or pastor the choice of walking away from this relationship and freeing the person you say you love to find a partner who is more compatible with his or her view of how to approach life. Your differences can either enhance or destroy your love and your future together. If you can find ways to bridge the differences, your view of life will be expanded and enhanced. If you move forward but do not address your differences, these will become your undoing.

Dialogue on your differences—it will make a difference!

 Perspective

- My pace of life:
- My temperament style:
- My conflict-resolution style:
- My love language:
- My birth order:
- My relax-and-recharge style:
- My spiritual gift(s):
- My parenting style:

Perspective

- My pace of life:
- My temperament style:
- My conflict-resolution style:
- My love language:
- My birth order:
- My relax-and-recharge style:
- My spiritual gift(s):
- My parenting style:

 *Love Chat*

- The difference that will most enhance and enrich our life together:
- The difference that left unaddressed could potentially undo our love:
- What we need to do that will maximize our differences and work *for* us:
- What we need to do to bridge the potential pitfalls of our differences and protect our love with a tangible plan to address these differences positively:

DATE *to* DISCOVER

Take the most likely area of potential conflict and create a date to help bridge the gap. Attend a seminar, take an online test or inventory, listen to a Christian leader's video or podcast, or read a book together on that topic.

Go out with a couple who seem like a mismatch but are in love. Ask what the secret was for them to bridge the gap in their differences.

A Little Adam & Eve Humor

What is one of the first things Adam and Eve did after they were kicked out of the Garden? They raised a little Cain.

Adam was returning home late one night after drinking with the dodo and the unicorn. Eve got angry and yelled at him, "You are seeing another woman!"

Adam responded, "Don't be silly. You are the only woman on earth," and went to sleep.

Later that night Adam woke up feeling a tickle in his chest and saw it was Eve.

"What are you doing?" he asked.

"I'm counting your ribs," she said.

4

Are We Making Progress?

Develop Habits of Growth

*Happy marriages begin when we marry the one we love,
and they blossom when we love the one we married.* [1]

$\mathcal{R}$elationships do not remain static. They develop and change as new information is discovered. For this reason, a healthy relationship is one that is clearly defined and operates socially, emotionally, and physically within the boundaries of its current definition.

We see people regularly make three mistakes when it comes to defining relationships. The first is they don't define them. They feel their way through relationships trying to discern from their emotions how they should treat the people in their lives. We don't want to discount the influence of emotions because they are a good thing. Emotions add energy to life and make our decisions more effective by raising our motivation. Emotions will give you courage to do what you know you ought to do. They assist us on our journey, but they are not equipped to be our guides. When we turn over the direction of our lives to the whims of our emotions, we guarantee unpredictable outcomes.

Second, people neglect to ask the question, "Are we at the same level of commitment or development in our relationship?" Relationships are a matter of the heart so they involve strong emotions and intense personal desires. At the same time, few of us get any real training in how relationships work so we are novices at how to guide these powerful forces. We have an instinctive sense that we ought to be at similar levels of personal investment in the relationship if it is going to succeed, so we make assumptions about the other person rather than actually discussing the subject in a rational and intentional way. They simply let their relationships operate accidentally and hope for the best.

You may accidentally land at the same place and be amazed at how it works out. You may just as easily end up as an accident that leaves behind shattered dreams and a broken heart.

Third, some people who believe it is important to define relationships overwork the issue and overanalyze every aspect. Check out the following examples we have encountered of questions that create an awkward atmosphere that defeats almost every possibility for healthy relationships.

- Among a circle of friends, a young man announced, "I just want everyone to know that I am going to get married as a virgin. If any of you don't agree with that conviction, please let me know now so I don't waste time asking you out."

- A young lady had a habit of asking new prospects on the first date, "Do you have intentions of marrying me? Because if you do there are a lot of things I need you to know about me and I need to know about you."

- After three dates, Don asked Sally, "What kind of relationship do you think we have?" After five dates, he asked, "What kind of relationship do you think we have?" After seven dates, he asked the same thing. It got to be such a habit that Sally became convinced he was going to ask this question every time they got together. She finally asked, "Why do you keep asking me that question?" She knew it wasn't going to work out when he responded, "I'm just making sure you don't change your mind. That would devastate me."

- Steven was surprised when Becky became suspicious shortly after they got engaged. "Do you think that girl is prettier than I am? Are you really committed to me or are you just stringing me along? You probably wouldn't be satisfied with just me anyway, would you?" The first time she asked this, Steven chalked it up to insecurity. When it began to happen every time they got together, he concluded it was a mistake to get engaged and he called off the wedding.

It is a good thing to define your important relationships, but overworking it makes you seem desperate and insecure while it pushes others out of your life.

Levels of Involvement

In simplest terms, there are five levels of personal involvement in any relationship. Each level is progressively more revealing, vulnerable, and dedicated. Your personal level of investment can be cautious, curious, confident, connected, or committed. When it comes to dating and courting, it is wise for you to determine the level of attachment for both you and your partner. Review the brief descriptions below to help you determine where your commitment stands.

Cautious relationships operate at the level of acquaintances. Conversation is limited to vacations, hobbies, tasks at work, and anything about yourself you would be willing to share on a cable news program. Topics such as your dreams, fears, and disappointments are avoided because there is not sufficient trust in the friendship. At this level of involvement, too much disclosure and intimate physical contact breeds awkwardness, insecurity, and conflict.

Curious relationships operate at the level of work colleagues and casual friendships. There is a sense that this could grow, so we share a little more to see if we can truly trust. You like spending time with these people as you see value in either being productive together or playing together. These are good relationships for getting tasks done, but they aren't positioned to handle intimacy well. Like cautious relationships, this level of involvement grows hesitant and uncomfortable with too much disclosure or physical contact.

Confident relationships operate at the level of trusted friends and exclusive dating interests. We talk freely, share personally, and generally trust these people with all but the deepest areas of our lives. We still hold back in these relationships because we aren't sure they can handle the raw reality of our shortcomings and deficiencies. We, therefore, put our best foot forward and allow others to look good around us. These friendships are extremely valuable to us, but by their nature, they lack the capacity to sustain a lifelong, intimate relationship. These relationships can handle a high level of verbal and emotional disclosure, but they tend to become insecure if physical contact goes beyond what is appropriate in a deep friendship.

Connected relationships are those you have with mentors and the person you are engaged to. These are people you trust to help you become a better person. Mentors give you advice and instruction based on input from you on what your needs and obstacles are. A fiancé or fiancée is someone you believe is a good choice for a life partner so you are willing to intensely explore the relationship. In essence, you test these relationships to see if they have what it takes. These relationships can handle a high degree of disclosure and vulnerability.

It is easy to conclude that it is all right to take the limits off physical expressions of love when you are engaged because you think, *We are going to get married anyway.* We believe it is best to wait until marriage for full sexual expression since this is an important time of evaluation. Up until now, you have been somewhat cautious with each other because you weren't sure if the other person could handle the full slate of your convictions and quirks. During the engagement period, you are going to reveal more of these, which will force you to ask, *Can I really live with this person for the rest of my life?* Sexual interaction makes it nearly impossible to do this sort of evaluation with honest clarity.

Committed relationships operate at the level of a married couple. We share everything in our lives from our living quarters, the bed, the budget, our bodies, our skills, and our imperfections. We make life-altering decisions together, and we build a life of investments, hard work, and family heritage. At this level, your heart is invested in the relationship to the point that your greatest joys, hurts, expectations, and insecurities are exposed to the other person. As a result, you would do almost anything to make the relationship work.

On the chart below, put an *X* in the box that best represents your level of personal involvement in your relationship. Then put an *X* in the box that represents the level of personal involvement your partner has in your relationship. Then in the last column briefly describe why you placed the mark at the level you chose.

HIS Perspective

Level of Involvement	Cautious	Curious	Confident	Connected	Committed	Why I marked it this way
My Involvement						
My Partner's (as I perceive it)						

Her Perspective

Level of Involvement	Cautious	Curious	Confident	Connected	Committed	Why I marked it this way
My Involvement						
My Partner's (as I perceive it)						

 *Love Chat*

Now compare your responses. Ideally, you will have placed your *X*s at the same level. If there are differences, have a courageous discussion about why.

Stages of Development

When it comes to romantic interests in your life, there are five stages of development these relationships go through. These stages help you to determine if your relationship has what it takes to progress from the curious to the committed level of involvement. Just as an individual goes through stages of growth and development, intimate relationships need to progress through various stages of maturity in order to prepare for a lifetime of love.

Once you have decided that your relationship is worthy of romantic interest, it is wise to determine which stage of development it is currently at. Then, it will serve you well to ask yourself if you believe this relationship has what it takes to progress through all the stages over time. It is common for relationships to get stuck at certain stages of development as an announcement to you that it is not supposed to progress further.

A lot of people in this world have some of the characteristics you find most attractive. It is possible, therefore, for you to be attracted to people who are not intended to be your life partner. These relationships will stall somewhere along the way, indicating it is time to release each other. Researchers use different terms to refer to these stages, but most agree there are five of them.

1. Interest

This is the beginning point of any romantic relationship. You may be attracted by physical characteristics because most of us have a certain body type we are drawn to. You may also be attracted to the pursuits you see this person involved with. If they are interested in activities or subjects that capture your heart, you will find time with this person an attractive option. This happens because we all have a sense of purpose, even if it is vague, and anyone who does things that connect to that purpose will stir interest in us. This is, of course, a superficial starting point and is no guarantee of future success.

2. Infatuation

At some point you decided you wanted to pursue a relationship. You learned just enough about the other person to believe you could trust him or her with the romantic longings of your heart. The infatuation stage begins as an intoxicating journey. You long to see each other. You laugh at each other's jokes, cry at each other's setbacks, and feel as if your soul mate might have appeared. Any time you interrupt each other's lives seems like a point of destiny and every interaction seems magical.

In this highly charged emotional environment, it is nearly impossible to rationally evaluate anything, let alone the strength of your relationship. This is one of the reasons we strongly encourage you not to engage in sexual activity at this level. We understand it is very easy to say yes to sex at this point because you are crazy about each other. You probably think this is the most attractive, most sensitive, most exciting person you have ever met. In fact, you probably struggle to see any flaws in this individual. If you begin to share your bodies sexually, it becomes even harder to remain objective when you enter the next phase of intimacy where you have to ask hard questions about you, your partner, and your relationship.

3. Investigation

If you continue to see each other, you will begin to wonder if this relationship is going to be a long-term venture. This natural inquisitiveness causes the relationship to change as you explore the issues that determine whether you have the potential for a lifelong relationship. During this phase, you will take inventory of your abilities and your deficiencies. The relationship takes a serious turn at this point as you become aware of your core values and you seek to determine if you are truly meant to be together. This can become a time of agonizing disequilibrium or joyful confirmation. Because this is the stage many reading this book will find themselves, we will spend a bit more time here.

During the investigation stage, you are seeking to determine if both of you have the ingredients upon which you can build a life together. You have already concluded that you can have fun together and enjoy each other's company. Now it is time to determine if you will be an effective team. You can have confidence in your ability as a couple if you observe sufficient maturity in your intellectual content, intentional character, interactive communication, and interested cooperation.

Intellectual Content

You will be asking important questions and facing intellectual challenges for the rest of your life. How do we navigate our careers? What contribution are we going to make to our generation? How are we going to raise children? What will we do when we face a tragedy, illness, or unexpected trauma? What is our plan for personal growth during the seasons of life ahead?

None of us can know ahead of time what life will bring, but we can determine if we have the intellectual agility to problem-solve together. Ask yourself the following questions to determine if you and your partner are intellectually mature enough for marriage:

Question	Him	Her
Do I actively learn something new each week?	❑ Yes ❑ No	❑ Yes ❑ No
Do I know how to research subjects I know little about?	❑ Yes ❑ No	❑ Yes ❑ No
Do I have a plan for intellectual growth for the next year?	❑ Yes ❑ No	❑ Yes ❑ No
Do I welcome the challenge of learning something new?	❑ Yes ❑ No	❑ Yes ❑ No
Do I get stressed or angry when faced with a new intellectual challenge?	❑ Yes ❑ No	❑ Yes ❑ No

Intentional Character

Marriage is unlike any other relationship because it links everything in your life with everything in your partner's life. As a result, it is more intense, more secure, and more uncomfortable than any other relationship. Most marriages lead to children, which causes your life to become bigger, more responsible, and more demanding.

Successful couples are prepared to grow as individuals so they can face the challenges as they arise. Although nobody can predict what life will bring, it is possible to develop confidence in your ability to make progress. A few basic character traits greatly increase your ability to deal with the reality of an adult life. Telling the truth, taking initiative, delaying gratification, and making healthy moral decisions are powerful predictors of future success. If you notice that your partner is deliberating seeking to develop these strengths, you can have confidence that you have chosen an effective partner. People without these traits tend to be short-sighted and ill-prepared for the growing realities of a family even though they are a lot of fun when responsibility is low. Let's look at these individually.

Telling the truth is vital if you are going to develop an atmosphere of trust. You can't know everything about each other because life is too complex for that, but if you are going to have confidence that your partner is trustworthy, you have to believe what they say. If there is a track record of truthfulness, your confidence will be high and vice versa. We told our kids that our first priority for them was to tell the truth. We told them they would get in more trouble for lying to us than anything else because we wanted to be able to trust them.

It does need to be said that tactfulness and truthfulness are best served together. It is possible to be brutally honest to the point that you wound the one you love. Your intentions may be correct and sincere, but that doesn't mean you are skilled in telling the truth. For instance, saying:

- "You are getting fat and should really take better care of yourself," may be true, but it is unlikely to be helpful.

- "What you just said was stupid. Where did you come up with that?" may be true, but we are pretty sure it will not add value to your relationship.

The goal of truthfulness is not to be right all the time but to build a foundation of believability in your relationship. Nobody says the right thing every time, and we ought to maintain a healthy sense of humor over the times we put our foot in our mouth.

I (Bill) was having a great time with Pam not too long ago. We were laughing and getting caught up with each other as we shared stories of the week. Then, for some unknown reason, I blurted out something that was just really insensitive. It was one of those moments when you realize just a little too late that what you are saying is not going to accomplish anything good. I was stunned at myself because I wasn't trying to be mean. There are times, to be sure, when my attitude is childish and I say things with a little bite in them, but this wasn't one of those. I was enjoying Pam's company and I wasn't aware of anything that was bugging me.

Without hesitation, I followed up the insensitive comment with, "I can't believe I just said that. That was so insensitive. I obviously wasn't thinking because I would never have planned to say what I just said."

I looked at Pam and could tell she was a little stunned also, so I kept talking. "Really, Pam, I can't believe I just said that. I don't even believe the words that came out of my mouth. That was so weird. I didn't even have time to reel them back in, they just blurted out like they had a mind of their own. Whoa, that was really insensitive."

Fortunately, my rambling rescued the mood. What could have been a hurtful, lingering memory got us both laughing. Pam gave me the benefit of the doubt because I have a long enough track record of sensitivity toward her, and she accepts that the tongue has a mind of its own and gets carried away sometimes.

It was a perfect example of James 3:2,10, "We all stumble in many ways. Anyone who is never at fault in what they say is perfect, able to keep their whole body in check...Out of the same mouth come praise and cursing. My brothers and sisters, this should not be."

So, what exactly did I say to Pam that was so insensitive? Well, it wasn't a good thing to say the first time and I am not foolish enough to repeat it. You will just have to imagine what it might have been based on your own experience.

People who are truthful demonstrate the following habits:

- They generally do what they say they will do.

- They humbly admit to their shortcomings.

- They apologize when they are wrong or inadvertently hurt someone else.

- They talk about issues during times of conflict rather than criticize the people involved.

- They willingly answer questions but aren't afraid to set up boundaries when others are pushing too hard.

Taking initiative is a necessary adult skill for anyone who plans to be responsible. Life is filled with unexpected challenges, possessions that need to be maintained, and things that fall apart. Those who are willing to do preventative maintenance and respond to the challenges as they arise will accumulate an impressive list of accomplishments. Those who wait for others to address the needs will consistently be surprised by their disappointments. You can recognize someone who takes initiative because they develop the following habits:

- They set goals.

- They do personal chores in a timely manner without being asked or reminded.

- They make lists of what needs to be done. These lists may be written down or carried in their mind, but the list exists.

- They volunteer to help when they recognize a need.

Delaying gratification appears to be an advanced skill today. We are bombarded with instant news, instant information, and instant entertainment with technological assistance. It is difficult in this environment to develop an attitude that says, "It is valuable to wait." The enemy of high-quality lives is the demand for *now*. We want maturity now. We want our meals now. We want the newest technology now. We want career success now. We want our intimate needs to be met now. We want possessions now. We want the wisdom that comes from years of experience now.

In some areas of life we can, of course, expect quick success and access to information. Some other areas, however, cannot be rushed no matter how advanced our tools become. You cannot rush a pregnancy or the raising of a child. You can't rush the development of leadership skills. You can't rush the insight that comes from twenty years in a career. You can't rush the recovery process from a serious illness.

In the cycle of your marriage, there will be times when you have to wait. After the birth of children, loving couples have to wait, sometimes for weeks, before they resume sexual interaction. A difficulty with a child or a parent may require you to be physically apart for an extended time. You may dream of a major purchase that does not fit in your current budget. If you have proven you know how to wait patiently and put off the reward for your decisions, these times of waiting will be okay. If you are impatient and have a habit of demanding that your needs be met now, you will be nearly impossible to live with.

You can recognize someone who can delay gratification because they have developed the following habits:

* They know how to say no.
* They plan for major purchases.
* They value the process of learning.
* They seek to meet other people's needs before they address their own.
* They talk about the value of waiting.

Making healthy moral decisions proves that you are the real deal. We don't want to go too far with this because "all have sinned and fall short of the glory of God" (Romans 3:23). We have a Savior because we are all imperfect, so we don't want to mistake morality with a pursuit of perfection. The issue here is to try to discern the condition of the heart. A partner who loves sincerely from the heart is going to be a joy to live with. The relationship will be characterized by dependability, mutual respect, and guilt-free passion.

Unhealthy moral decisions, on the other hand, weaken everything they come in contact with. Organizations are weakened by the immoral financial decisions of their leaders. Families are weakened by overly critical and controlling parents. Love relationships are weakened by self-serving sexual decisions. And people's health is often weakened by foolish moral decisions that usher in addictions, STDs, and other calamities.

One of our sons has taken up mountain biking and decided to explore a new trail. It had snowed a couple of weeks before and temperatures had been fluctuating from midtwenties at night to high forties during the day. He failed to take into account that the slowly melting snow would impact the trail. When I asked how the ride went, he said, "I didn't get very far. So much mud accumulated in my tires that they stopped moving. It was so thick I had to pick mud and rocks out of the tread. I finally had to just turn around, find a hose, and ride home on the streets."

This experience represents the choices we all have in our moral lives. In this world, mud accumulates. Temptation is rampant and the opportunities to make mistakes abound. If we respond when there is just a little mud in the tires, it's not too difficult to deal with. "If we confess our sins, he is faithful and just and will forgive us our sins and purify us from all unrighteousness" (1 John 1:9). We can "hose off" and get back to healthy living without too much effort or agony.

When a lot of mud gums up the works, significant decisions are necessary to get back on track. "Come near to God and he will come near to you. Wash your hands, you sinners, and purify your hearts, you double-minded" (James 4:8). If our son had stubbornly kept going, he would have had a very long day. He could have dug the mud out of his tires, ridden a few feet, and then repeated the process, but it would have exhausted him. The best thing for him to do was to turn around, learn from the misadventure, and be wiser next time.

We all battle with desires that lead us to unproductive and unhealthy paths. The real test is how we respond. Do we willingly confess and repent or do we stubbornly refuse to make changes when change is obvious?

You can recognize someone with healthy moral character because they practice the following habits:

- They are actively involved in pursuits that promote personal growth.
- They have a strong friendship circle.
- They believe sexuality is a gift to be valued not a commodity to be consumed.
- They clearly state their convictions.
- They treat the opposite gender with respect.
- They are the same in private as they are in public.

On the chart below, rate yourself and your partner on the various areas of intentional character. For each trait, give a score from 1 to 5 with 5 meaning sufficient dependability to be held up as a role model and 1 meaning a significant deficiency in this area.

HIS Perspective

How mature are we with intentional character?	Him	Her
Telling the truth	1 2 3 4 5	1 2 3 4 5
Taking initiative	1 2 3 4 5	1 2 3 4 5
Delaying gratification	1 2 3 4 5	1 2 3 4 5
Making healthy moral decisions	1 2 3 4 5	1 2 3 4 5

Perspective

How mature are we with intentional character?	Him					Her				
Telling the truth	1	2	3	4	5	1	2	3	4	5
Taking initiative	1	2	3	4	5	1	2	3	4	5
Delaying gratification	1	2	3	4	5	1	2	3	4	5
Making healthy moral decisions	1	2	3	4	5	1	2	3	4	5

Interactive Communication

Since marriage is a partnership that includes financial decisions, romantic pursuits, time commitments, and the building of a legacy, your ability to negotiate with each other is a vital skill. It won't take you long to figure out that you are better at some things than your partner and vice versa. To maximize your experience, you are going to have to learn how to respect each other's strengths and fill in for each other's weaknesses. If you actively interact with one another, you will prove that you can problem-solve and adjust to whatever life brings your way.

Many people don't like to interact. They prefer to tell others what to do and intimidate them into submission. Others quietly appear to be agreeable but then get stubborn at critical moments. Someone who is too compliant today will grow resentful later on. Someone who actively negotiates and seeks to collaborate will lead when he possesses wisdom, but he will humbly follow when he recognizes another with more wisdom.

Interested Cooperation

Teamwork requires individuals who want to work as a team rather than have their way every time. Those who welcome other people's opinions, seek the wisdom others can bring, and value the strength that comes from networking together will prove to be valuable partners in life. Those who are consistently jealous of other people's success, critical of other's insights and decisions, or afraid of others taking advantage of them will eventually become a drain to your relationship and future success.

HIS Perspective

On the line below put an *M* (for male) to represent where you think you are on the scale of cooperative interaction. Then place an *F* (for female) to represent where you think your love interest is on the same scale.

Controlling	Compliant	Cooperative

Her Perspective

On the line below put an *F* (for female) to represent where you think you are on the scale of being cooperative interaction. Then place an *M* (for male) to represent where you think your love interest is on the same scale.

Controlling	Compliant	Cooperative

Hopefully, your confidence in your love for each other will increase as you investigate your potential as a couple. It's not easy to do this kind of evaluation because it forces your love to mature and become a little soberer. This is the stage where your objective understanding must integrate with your emotional connection. If your partner's character seems suspect under investigation, the emotional attraction that ignited your relationship will do battle with objective logic. You will be deeply drawn to this person while you grow suspicious of the future success of the relationship. If, on the other hand, your partner's character and conduct are consistent with your core values, your confidence in the relationship will increase and your attraction will grow deeper and more secure.

Wake-up Moments

The investigation phase begins to open us up to these topics and make us more self-aware. Lucia was madly in love with Rafael. They had dated for seven months and shared long walks in the park, lingering dinners filled with fascinating conversation, and many romantic adventures. He seemed like the perfect man, and she often found herself thinking, *I have found my soul mate. I didn't really want to entertain thoughts that there was someone out there who was perfect for me, but I truly believe I have found him.* She always wanted a partner she could communicate with, and he seemed willing to talk about anything. She wanted someone who valued her organizational abilities and commitment to a clean, healthy environment, and Rafael seemed impressed with everything she did. She dreamed of a man who would help her overcome her fears and pursue her dreams. Rafael was the safest refuge she had ever met.

In the eighth month of their relationship, she began to see another side of herself that affected the way she viewed Rafael. Whenever her stress level rose, she would instinctively talk faster and become more demanding of everyone around her. Fear would grip her heart and she would just start talking. It didn't seem to be an issue early on because Rafael patiently listened to her and sensitively responded. So she was shocked one night when he asked, "Are you always going to be like this?"

"Like what?" she asked.

"Are you going to tell me what to do for the rest of our lives?"

She couldn't believe it. The man who had respected everything she said for more than half a year was now so rude. He obviously didn't understand her or her concern for him, their life together, or the important causes in her life. Or maybe she was overreacting and was too directive with others when she felt stressed. She hadn't ever asked these questions before. Was Rafael the wrong choice for her and would he end up being consistently rude as time passed? Or was he exactly what she needed to face her fears and learn to be more balanced during times of stress?

Just as suddenly, she became aware that Rafael wasn't very concerned about cleanliness. His car was clean but not nearly as neatly kept as her vehicle. There were dishes in his sink most of the time. She had assumed it was because he was spending so much with her, but now she wondered if this was just the way he was. He also was content to leave clothes in the laundry basket for weeks, which she assumed was because he lived alone. Now she wasn't so sure.

Courageous Conclusions

Trent thought Tina was the most beautiful woman he had ever met. Their relationship started with a whirlwind of creative dates and fun activities. Her laugh was captivating, their conversations were fascinating, and her responses to him were full of love and encouragement. He truly believed he had met an angel.

As they were planning for the first anniversary of their dating life, he began to notice new traits emerging in her. She reacted in anger when he suggested an idea that was different from hers. She was offended when he suggested they get together with friends to have a celebration dinner. Out of nowhere she began to have an opinion about everything in his life. She thought he was working the wrong job. Then she evaluated his wardrobe and tried to convince him to get rid of most of what he owned and go on a shopping spree with her. When she launched into a lengthy critique of his family, he questioned for the first time if she was the right one for him.

He didn't realize before this how much he valued peace in his home and didn't like controversy. He had a big heart for the people who were important to him. He knew his family wasn't perfect, but he loved having them in his life and he needed a partner who valued his family as much as he did, warts and all.

During this vital stage, a couple decides if they have what it takes to build a life together. They have already proven they are attracted to each other and have enough chemistry to build on. The unanswered questions now are about compatibility and character. It is normal during this stage to ask questions such as:

> Does my partner believe the same as I do about God?
>
> Does my partner have the same moral values I have?
>
> Can we raise children together?
>
> Will it be safe for me physically, emotionally, and socially with this person?
>
> Can we make significant life decisions together or will we just argue with each other?
>
> Is my partner's anger level acceptable to me?
>
> Will my partner cooperate with me financially and domestically?
>
> What will I do if the habits I don't find attractive never change?

Terrific Turmoil

It was difficult for Lucia to admit that she became controlling and stubborn when she felt stress. She wanted to blame Rafael, but she knew deep in her soul that this was more about her than it was about him. The turmoil she experienced over this surprised her. She was willing to admit intellectually that this was an unhealthy trait. Somehow, saying it out loud was too vulnerable. Instead, her reactions to Rafael made it appear she was trying to push him away:

> "Why don't you ever clean your car before you pick me up for dates? I would not want my kids to ride in this car."
>
> "I'm not sure I can trust you. If you really wanted this to work, you would pay for all our dates rather than let me offer."
>
> "You make me so mad. I could never be married to a man who is angry. A man who gets angry scares me." (It didn't escape her notice that she was angry when she said this.)

She expected Rafael to give up on her even though she silently hoped he would accept her and stay strong in the midst of her tirades. She was coming to grips with the need to change these traits in herself and realized it would be easier to do in a loving, supportive relationship. Logically, she told herself it would be best if she admitted this to Rafael and quit being so hard on him, but her emotions would take over whenever she was with him.

Rafael could tell Lucia was overreacting to just about everything. He wanted to be compassionate, but the experience was irritating. He thought long and hard about whether he wanted to do this for the rest of his life. The decision was not obvious because he was a better man around her than he had been on his own. He was more focused, more aware of other's needs, and more patient. He also admired her skills in setting goals, organizing schedules, and managing finances, which he knew would be good additions to his life.

"Lucia, I'm not sure I can do this," he eventually said. "I love you and I think we are good together most of the time, but I feel like I'm being criticized, accused, and pushed away too much. I'm open to working this out, but I need to know if it will be like this forever. Because if you really are not happy with who I am, I think we should let each other go."

"Oh Rafael, I am so sorry," Lucia said. "You are the best man I've ever met, and I've been afraid to let you see who I really am. Being around you has shown me things about myself I had successfully hidden from myself. If we stay together, I won't be able to ignore these any longer, and I was afraid you might not be patient with me. So, I guess I was trying to push you away before you pushed me away."

Rafael and Lucia had a number of honest conversations about the areas where they needed to become more mature. Their relationship lost a little of its happiness but gained a depth of confidence as they took a good look at the more serious issues they needed to face to build a life together.

This is the strategic goal of the investigation stage of an intimate relationship. Attraction and chemistry are certainly necessary ingredients for a loving couple, but they must be mixed with resilient compassion that can absorb the imperfections a couple brings to the relationship and gently promote growth in each other. This type of camaraderie can be developed only through honest self-disclosure and courageous acceptance.

Recognize What Is Real

Trent and Tina didn't fare quite so well. The harder Trent tried to persuade Tina that his family needed to be an important part of their lives, the more she resisted. Negotiating the Thanksgiving holiday that year was disappointing to Trent.

He suggested, "I think we should visit my family on Friday since we're going to spend all day Thursday with your family."

He was shocked when Tina shot back, "My mom and my sisters always go shopping on Friday after Thanksgiving. Your family doesn't do anything. In fact, they never do anything worthwhile."

Trent ended up seeing his family on Friday by himself while Tina joined in with her family. The bad taste in his mouth turned into a disaster when the Christmas holiday came up for discussion.

"Tina, I need us to talk about when we're going to see my family during Christmas. We have a family tradition of getting together on Christmas Eve, which I'd really like us to participate in."

This touched off something in Tina that Trent still doesn't understand. She was immediately offended and started criticizing the members of his family. "Peter doesn't care about anyone but himself. Your mom pries into everyone's business, and I don't think she likes me. Your dad just sits around watching TV and ignores everyone else. I sure hope you aren't going to turn out to be like him. Just the thought of spending time with them stresses me out."

It seemed to Trent she could have gone on forever with negative comments about the people he cared most about. As his heart sank, he stopped talking because he knew it was over. She wasn't catching on that his family needed to have a place in his life and the life of anyone he would marry. He knew he would need to limit the time and access his family would get so he could make his wife a priority, but he was not willing to cut them out of his life completely. Even though he thought she was remarkable and beautiful, he knew this was a deal breaker.

"Tina, I'm sorry but this is not going to work out. I can't be with someone who is this critical of my family."

"What are you talking about? I love your family, and they are going to learn so much when I'm a part of your life."

"That is what I'm talking about. My family will never live up to your expectations, and I can tell this is going to be something we argue over for the rest of our lives, and I cannot do that."

The break-up was difficult as Tina turned her criticisms on Trent. She used to be so proud of him, but now she couldn't seem to find anything good in him. Every negative comment strengthened his resolve. They had plenty of attraction to each other, but their habits and expectations could not withstand the investigation stage as they took a long-term look at their potential.

Passionate Clarity

If it hasn't occurred to you yet, sexual involvement prior to this stage significantly complicates your ability to objectively evaluate your potential as a couple. Sexual interaction releases chemicals that promote strong connections between the two of you. No other activity on earth is as physically vulnerable as getting naked with another person and stimulating the sexual organs. To think that after sharing that level of physical intimacy you can then objectively and logically ask questions about long-term compatibility and cooperation is comparable to buying and driving a beautiful and expensive car before you have a driver's license. It may turn out well for you, but you are taking a big risk.

4. Investment

As you progress through the investigation stage, you will reach a key decision-making moment. If your confidence in the relationship is high enough, you will set your heart to spend the rest of your life with the person you have been evaluating. At this point, your reservations take a back seat and your heart becomes willing to commit yourself without hesitation. You will view everything differently from this point forward. Decisions become moments to rejoice together about the life you will share. Conflicts become opportunities for growth and clarification.

You know you are at the investment stage in your love for another person when:

- You are willing to share your money.

- You have a strong desire to make your most important decisions together.

- You are willing to talk about any subject without fear.

- You are confident you could love this person even if they were in an accident, suffered a disability, or faced a life-changing illness.

- You are confident you will be loved just as much even if you gain weight, get older, or slow down physically.

- You believe in your heart you can face any challenge together.

- You welcome input from your partner on how you can become a better person.

- You are confident you will raise your kids with similar convictions, expectations, and goals.

Before we discuss interdependence, the fifth stage of development in an intimate relationship, let's have you consider your decisions about what physical expressions of love are appropriate at each stage.

We Make Our Choices, Our Choices Make Us

In the beatitudes, Jesus said, "Blessed are the pure in heart for they shall see God" (Matthew 5:8). Picture sexuality as a continuum. At one end of the spectrum is holding hands, while sexual intercourse and oral sex form the other end. We know from 1 Thessalonians 4:3 that it is God's will for you to abstain from sexual immorality (which means any sex outside the context of marriage). So God knows that to stay pure in heart you have to move your line before oral sex and intercourse. But how far back from that do you need to push the line to maintain your ability to "see God" or maintain your own pure heart and protect the purity of those you date?

If sexual intercourse is out of God's will until marriage, then the things that prepare your body to give and receive sex are a dangerous, slippery slope. Foreplay of stimulating sexual organs under clothes or over clothes are all a part of the sexual dance. It makes sense that the line of purity is back far in advance of this act of sexual foreplay.

But how far back should your line be at each stage of your relationship? For some, making out sets them up to desire sexual intercourse. Others seem to feel they can handle extended making out and kissing sessions and not fall into sexual temptation. The majority of people, though, long for more and more, and keep pushing the edge once make-out sessions begin. Some seem to be able to handle a few kisses and maintain a pure heart. Others, once they begin kissing, move right into making out and then foreplay within minutes. Some can handle a good-night kiss or a greeting kiss. Some can kiss after prayer together and maintain a pure heart. Still others will find that any kissing, even one, lights the fires of passion. The key to success is to know yourself so you can wisely set your personal boundaries. What we see is that most people fail because they are not honest *with themselves*, let alone honest with the person they are dating.

Below you will see a chart with various ways of expressing romantic love through physical acts. It is simpler to progress through the stages if your physical activity is consistent with your level of involvement. Place the words *Interest, Infatuation, Investigation, Investment,* and *Interdependence* at the place you think is appropriate for each stage.

How far am I willing to go?

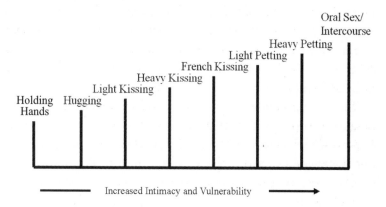

5. Interdependence

Over time, successful couples find a balance between their individual pursuits, family responsibilities, and their personal relationship. Nobody gets married because they want to be busy and have their lives interrupted by kids, bills, and demanding community involvements. It is, however, the reality of an adult life.

It is nearly impossible to reach the interdependence stage of development during dating, courtship, and engagement, but it is important to ask if you see the potential in your possible future mate to adjust to the selfless nature of a responsible adult. There is an exception for those couples who are coming into the marriage with children of their own. By the nature of their life circumstances, they are forced to be more responsible than a single individual with no children.

This stage is a distressing time for many couples because it is not fun or casual. As a married couple, you have to get up every morning and go to work. You have to get up a lot of nights because of children who are scared, restless, or sick. You have to focus on your family relationships at the end of a busy workday with an attitude that says, "I am glad you are in my life." Dads and moms adopt a "do what we need to do" approach at this time because life is strenuous, and they have no other choice. Gary Brainerd notes, "While most parents are loathe to acknowledge it, the painful truth is that children require a lot of energy as do jobs and careers." [2] As a result, it is common for couples to report a relatively low level of satisfaction during this stage of their journey.

Part of successfully navigating this stage is the willing development of individual pursuits. It is hard to think romantically about each other when you are up late at night with a sick child. It is unreasonable to dream about each other when you are working through a pressure situation at work. Intimacy at this stage means you believe in each other and in your ability to face down the challenges of life. Success also requires a more deliberate and mature approach to love and romance. Scheduling dates, vacations, romantic rendezvous, and sexual encounters becomes necessary while spontaneous opportunities become scarce.

The family business meeting where schedules and purchases are lined out becomes a mandate that nobody really enjoys but everyone needs to embrace. These are not the things short-term dreams are made of. They are, however, the stuff long-term legacies are built upon. For that reason, couples who stick to it tend to report high levels of relationship satisfaction later in life after their children have grown up.

Again, it isn't realistic for you to observe your partner in this phase of life before you get married, but it is wise to discern if the two of you have what it takes, not just to be happy, but to work through the rigors of an adult life together by asking:

Perspective

- Does my work ethic match the size of the goals I say I want to accomplish?
- Am I willing to do domestic chores with a good attitude?
- Do inconveniences make me angry to the point of being destructive to my relationships?
- Am I experienced at delayed gratification? Do I feel strong when I delay purchases, personal preferences, sexual urges, and fun activities for higher priorities?
- Am I humble enough to believe that sometimes the woman I love is right? Can I think of any examples where I said, "Wow, she is much smarter about that than I am"?

Perspective

- Does my work ethic match the size of the goals I say I want to accomplish?
- Am I willing to do domestic chores with a good attitude?
- When my partner is not able to help me with something I think is important, do I get angry with him or do I applaud him for his hard work and attention to personal growth?
- Am I experienced at sharing control? When I feel emotionally strong about something, do I humbly negotiate or do I use my emotions to get others to do what I want?
- Am I secure enough to accept constructive criticism from people I don't want to disappoint?
- Am I humble enough to believe that sometimes the man I love is right? Can I think of any examples where I said, "Wow, he is much smarter about that than I am"?

HIS Evaluation

Below you will find three charts for rating what stage of development you think your relationship is in. On the first chart, mark the stage where you are in the relationship. On the second chart, mark where you think your partner is in the relationship. On the third chart, ask your most trusted friends to give their opinion of where each of you is in the relationship.

I am at the following stage of development in our relationship:				
Interest	Infatuation	Investigation	Investment	Interdependence

I think my partner is at the following stage of development in our relationship:				
Interest	Infatuation	Investigation	Investment	Interdependence

My friends think we are at the following stage of development in our relationship:					
	Interest	Infatuation	Investigation	Investment	Interdependence
Me					
My Partner					

Evaluation

Below you will find three charts for rating what stage of development you think your relationship is in. On the first chart, mark the stage where you are in the relationship. On the second chart, mark where you think your partner is in the relationship. On the third chart, ask your most trusted friends to give their opinion of where each of you is in the relationship.

I am at the following stage of development in our relationship:				
Interest	Infatuation	Investigation	Investment	Interdependence

I think my partner is at the following stage of development in our relationship:				
Interest	Infatuation	Investigation	Investment	Interdependence

My friends think we are at the following stage of development in our relationship:					
	Interest	Infatuation	Investigation	Investment	Interdependence
Me					
My Partner					

DATE *to* DISCOVER

Go on a date to plan some future dates that will be markers in your relationship. For example:

Interest: Try a new hobby together (cooking class, a sport, art class).

Infatuation: Attend an event (such as a wedding, a ball or dance, or concert) that sparks the flirty and fun side of a relationship.

Investigation: Attend a relationship seminar, marriage class, or have dinner with a mentor couple. Learn how others investigate their own compatibility and calling into a relationship.

Investment: Stay overnight at a family member's home or go on a family vacation (make sure you make plans for separate accommodations to safeguard against any temptation for sexual activity). Any time you are with family, this builds relationship awareness, deepens the relationship bond, and your family will be making an investment into the relationship too.

Interdependence: Go on a date that builds into a shared future, such as shopping for furniture, looking at rings, and attending a real-estate open house.

A Little Adam *&* Eve Humor

Adam to Eve: "I'll wear the plants in this family!"

Can We Handle Our Families?

Choose to Love Yours, Mine, and Ours

*May there be a generation of children
on the children of your children.*[1]

*O*ne of the most personal questions you will ever ask as a couple is, "How will we get along with our families after we get married?" We know this is a very sensitive area because of all the tension-filled in-law stories floating around.

> George went on a vacation to the Middle East with most of his family, including his mother-in-law. During their vacation, and while they were visiting Jerusalem, George's mother-in-law died. With the death certificate in hand, George went to the American Consulate Office to make arrangements to send the body back to the States for proper burial.
>
> The Consul, after hearing of the death of the mother-in-law, told George, "My friend, the sending of a body back to the States for burial is very, very expensive. It could cost as much as $5,000 dollars." The Consul continued, "In most of these cases, the person responsible for the remains normally decides to bury the body here. This would only cost $150 dollars."

George thought for some time, and answered the Consul, "I don't care how much it will cost to send the body back. That's what I want to do."

The Consul, after hearing this said, "You must have loved your mother-in-law very much, considering the difference in price between $5,000 and $150 dollars."

"No, it's not that," says George. "You see, I know of a case many, many years ago of a person that was buried here in Jerusalem, and on the third day he was resurrected. Consequently, I do not want to take that chance!" [2]

It's a Family Affair

For the most part, your relationship is about you as a couple, but in many ways you really do marry each other's families. The people who raised you have made an enormous investment of time, money, and emotional energy in your lives. As a result, they are not very objective about you and they have a difficult time letting go of their opinions. In addition, they were the most influential people in your lives during your most impressionable years. Your basic character and your understanding of love were set in your heart during your first eight years of life by the people who loved you.

If the family you grew up in was skilled at relationships, this is good news because you will have strong instincts. If, however, your family was plagued with unhealthy interactions, it is going to take courageous actions and concerted focus to develop new, effective skills in your marriage.

The Evaluation

We must all courageously evaluate the health of the family we grew up in to keep making progress on our journey to maturity. This is at least part of the point of Genesis 2:24, "That is why a man leaves his father and mother and is united to his wife, and they become one flesh." This evaluation revolves around strategic questions related to our families:

- What traits from the family I grew up in do I want to repeat because they are healthy and encouraging?

- What traits from the family I grew up in need to be replaced in my new family because they were unhealthy?

- What new behaviors do I want to establish in my life to replace the traits that were unhealthy?

Epic Examples

Some of you have epic love stories of your family's heritage to build on. Be grateful if you have parents, grandparents, and great-grandparents who stayed married for life. Interview your married relatives and listen to the secrets of their successes. An attendee at one of our marriage conferences told us that her folks had been happily married over sixty years:

> My parents wanted a way to say "I love you" but without words, so they would squeeze hands three times meaning "I love you." It became a part of our family culture. We'd see them walk hand-in-hand and catch the three squeezes, or see them holding hands in church and see them squeeze three times. Or they might be walking with one of us kids or grandkids and squeeze our hand three times. Our family held hands during grace so we began to squeeze three times. At the end of Daddy's life, he couldn't talk. With his last breath, he reached across those white hospital sheets to squeeze Mother's hand three times, "I love you." Then he entered heaven.

That is epic love.

One of our favorite love stories came to us in our travels to build into military marriages. We had the opportunity to visit the Airborne and Special Operations Museum in Fayetteville, North Carolina. We were excited to learn about some of the heroes that have provided the freedoms we enjoy. Little did we know the museum housed an incredibly romantic story.

Eugene Deibler Jr. pooled money with two of his friends to buy a $100 car after being stationed at Camp McCall during World War II. Together they planned an outing to a local lake, and one of his friends invited Mary Smith to come along as a companion for Eugene. The car had no air conditioning so it was rather miserable on the 105 degree day, and Eugene told his friend to be Mary's date because "it was too hot to be hospitable."

"She came walking down the steps," Eugene said. "I had never seen anything so beautiful in my life. She was gorgeous."

When she walked over to the car, she asked, "Where should I sit?"

"Right here, beside me," Eugene insisted.

Three weeks later, he asked her to marry him. "She said yes, but she wouldn't marry me before I went overseas. She said, 'If you come back, then we'll get married.'"

As a member of the 101st Airborne Division, Eugene Deibler was dropped into Normandy on June 6, 1944, to secure the area just inland hours before other D-Day troops came ashore. When he hit the ground, he used his knife to cut off as much of his reserve chute as he could stuff in his pack. When he returned to England at the end of July, he mailed the silk to Mary with a note that told her it was for her bridal gown.

Mary Smith wore the dress she made from his parachute on December 22, 1945, during a ceremony in the living room of her parents' house. The dress is now on display in the museum as a memorial to their epic love. They were married for sixty-one years, but their story will inspire generations to come.

Unfortunately, not all of us have a legacy of love handed down to us through our families. Some of us have to be the first to create that legacy.

When some friends of ours took over their first pastorate at an inner-city church, they realized they were the *only* married couple in their church. There were lots of babies, lots of relationships, but no one was married—they all just had "baby daddies." In one family, for five generations back no one was married. The natural outcome was a cycle of devastating poverty, which this pastor and his wife were determined to change. They realized there were no instant answers, but they believed they could help the next generation begin a healthy legacy.

Every year now they run decision-making programs for kids and teens that include a strong emphasis on lifelong marriage, sexual integrity, and legacy building. When they are asked, "Why should I do this? My momma didn't do this and we are okay," their answer is, "God wants you to be more than okay. He wants you to begin a legacy."

If you come from a family with a history of cohabitation or common-law relationships, you will need to be courageous in your obedience to God's plan. You might need to surround yourself with other couples who have made the step of a marriage commitment. Invite people into your life who will celebrate your responsibility, maturity, and wisdom in taking the step of marriage.

Break the Barrier

Statistically, people tend to repeat the patterns of their families of origin. Children of divorce are more likely to get a divorce. Children raised in violence are more likely to be perpetrators or victims of domestic violence. Those who have a parent addicted to drugs, drinking, or gambling are more likely to have those same issues.

But thankfully, God's Spirit isn't handcuffed by statistics. If you are willing to take a good hard look in the mirror, confront the demons of your past, and slay them with God's power and God's Word, you can be set free to have a wonderful future filled with the love, joy, peace, patience, kindness, goodness, faithfulness, gentleness, and self-control that produce a lifetime of love (Galatians 5:22-23).

If this is an area of concern, you may want to create your own genogram. A trained counselor can help you through the process or you can explore various websites that provide software to help you build a visual history of your family's behavior patterns. [3] Below is a very simple genogram of part of our family. If statistics ruled, we would be the least likely couple to write a book on long-lasting love.

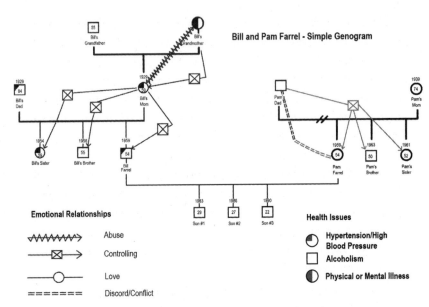

Bill and Pam Farrel - Simple Genogram

Emotional Relationships

∿∿∿∿∿→	Abuse
──⊠─→	Controlling
──○──	Love
══════	Discord/Conflict

Health Issues

◑	Hypertension/High Blood Pressure
☐	Alcoholism
◐	Physical or Mental Illness

You can see from the diagram that my (Bill's) mom was a difficult person to grow up with. She was afraid, angry, and attempted to control everything in her life as a way of protecting herself from the trauma she experienced during her teen years. Also, Pam's dad was difficult because of persistent alcoholism that brought out either depression or rage in him. When we looked at our families of origin, we had some obvious negative behaviors to deal with. It was harder to find the positive traits but, even amidst the chaos, we were able to uncover some great traits that were worth continuing into the next generation.

Pam's chart of things to keep and things to replace included the following:

Things to Keep: great work ethic (from grandfather, father, mother, grandmothers); loyalty and kindness toward family, friends, and neighbors (from mother, father, both sets of grandparents); belief in Jesus (mother); belief in "creator" (most of my family tree); integrity and honesty—"my word is my bond" (from mother, maternal grandparents, paternal grandmother); community and civic involvement (from mother, maternal grandparents, paternal grandmother).

Things to Replace: addiction to alcohol from my father, grand-father, and great-grandfather (Alcoholism is the sap of my family tree! I replaced it with the decision to never drink.); rage and domestic violence of my father (replaced with consistent spiritual growth, deliberate requests for the Holy Spirit to put peace in my heart, and a decision to whisper if I felt frustration rising); poverty caused by my paternal grandfather's lack of initiative (replaced with hard work, innovation, education, and inspiration of God's Spirit); codependency, shame, and victim mentality of my paternal grandmother and mother (replaced with healthy interdependence, discernment of healthy people, and trust of healthy leaders); sexual activity outside of marriage of many women in my family (replaced with a purity vow until I married, which I kept because it helped me see with my brain, not my hormones).

Bill's chart included the following:

Things to Keep: strong work ethic (from grandfather, father, and mother); simple sense of integrity (from my father—"If it is the right thing to do, you just do it"); love of career (from my dad, who said regularly, "I can't believe they pay me to do this"); creativity and a natural interest in innovation (from my mom); strong sense of morality.

Things to Replace: Most decisions were made out of fear because my mom was afraid of a long list of things (replaced with a deliberate decision-making process). Mom isolated our family as a way of maintaining control (replaced with consistent involvement in church and Bible studies). Dad was passive while my mom acted outlandishly (replaced with regular meetings with Pam to keep our life on the same page). Dad and Mom would yell, scream, and throw things in conflict (replaced with a deliberate conflict-resolution process). Mom underachieved and Dad was afraid of leadership (replaced with regular goal-setting exercises).

 *Love Chat*

Fill out the charts below with the traits you want to repeat and replace from the families you grew up in. Then share your insights with each other:

HIS Family

	EVALUATING THE TRAITS OF THE FAMILY I GREW UP IN	
	Traits I want to replace	
Traits I want to repeat	Description of old behavior	Description of new behavior

Her Family

	EVALUATING THE TRAITS OF THE FAMILY I GREW UP IN	
	Traits I want to replace	
Traits I want to repeat	Description of old behavior	Description of new behavior

Marriage Prime Time

Is there a prime time to marry? Your parents, siblings, friends, and leaders probably have an opinion about the right time to get married. In general, researchers agree that the midtwenties is the time of life with the greatest chance of success. Research by sociologist Norval Glenn of the University of Texas-Austin found that people who married between ages twenty-three and twenty-seven report greater satisfaction with their marriages and are less likely to break up than those who married earlier or later in life. [4] *Focus on the Family Findings* by Gary Stanton says that the prime age is twenty-two to twenty-five. Marrying at twenty-two increases the likelihood of couples marrying as virgins, which is an important factor in marital stability and happiness. Stanton concludes, "The 22 to 25 age-at-first-marriage range seems to be that which enhances both the quality and stability of marriage." [5] The biological clock is also a consideration: "Fertility researcher Richard Paulson of the University of Southern California says that, as a general rule, women should start having children no later than age 30 and be done by 35, when statistics show fertility declines." [6]

These are, of course, general guidelines that serve as good information to get you thinking. The real issue is maturity. Most people reach a level of maturity in their midtwenties that is compatible with an intimate, responsible relationship, but we all know exceptions. We married when we were twenty years old. Our oldest son married at twenty-one, but our middle son waited until twenty-five. And we probably all know people who are in midlife and still aren't ready for a committed relationship.

Some basic commonsense parameters can help you determine if you are mature enough to say, "I do":

- Do you have enough education to support yourself and your spouse?

- If you marry now, can you better achieve your goals and God's call on your life?

- Will marrying help you maintain your integrity?

The point is, *when it's time it's time!* Putting off getting married when you are sure is bound to interrupt other concerns. When we hear parents push off wedding dates simply because of money ("We can't afford a wedding"), we suspect priorities are askew. An actual wedding is inexpensive: a license, a pastor, and a place to wed (which can be a home or home church). It is the *party* that is expensive. If more time and energy are going into the wedding and reception than are being applied to premarital training and relational development, it is likely the couple will experience some difficult adjustments.

Relationship expert and pastor Mark Gungor says, "If young adult couples say they want to get married, parents should support them, even if they're still in college. How can we tell young people that living together and premarital sex lowers their chances for a happy marriage, and then say wait to marry until 28? What do you think you've just set up?" [7]

Should We Live Together?

The current age for the first marriage is higher than it has been since World War II, but not necessarily for a good reason. A 1946 Gallup poll found that most people considered the ideal age to be twenty-five for men and twenty-one for women. A Gallup poll sixty years later found the ideal age had increased to twenty-five for women and twenty-seven for men. [8] Premarital cohabitation contributed to the delay. From 1960 to 2011, the number of cohabitating couples jumped from 430,000 to 7.6 million. [9]

Often couples today opt for a cohabitating arrangement because they believe it is simpler and a safeguard that allows them to try out the relationship first. But living together is not the same as marriage. Before packing your bags and moving in together, consider these startling facts.

Children *are* affected. Among cohabiting couples, 40 percent also have children living in the household with them. Children born to cohabitating couples account for 27 percent of all births. These kids are at risk. In nonparental child-abuse cases, 84 percent are committed by the mother's boyfriend. According to the *Journal of Marriage and Family*, girls living in a home with a boyfriend (not a father or stepfather) are at a much higher risk for sexual abuse.

It's not a safe place for a woman. During a one-year period, thirty-five out of one hundred cohabitating couples experienced physical aggression. Domestic violence is twice as likely among live-in couples compared to married couples. In one study by the *Journal of Family Violence*, 48 percent of couples living together experienced domestic violence, compared to 19 percent of married couples and 27 percent of those divorced or separated. Studies indicate that relationships experience more violence when there is less societal and relational commitment. The marriage license does seem to be a shield of protection for many married women—most likely because the man in her life valued her enough to take the steps to express his commitment to her in a marriage ceremony.

Cohabitation sets you up for divorce. Those who live together prior to marriage are twice as likely to divorce if they do get married. And the longer the cohabitation, the more likely divorce is, according to sociologists at the University of Wisconsin. Those who live together separate more often if they do marry, and they also regard the relationship as a less important part of their life. It seems cohabitation trains couples to disregard the love relationship—just the opposite of what most couples cite as their reason for living together.

According to a UCLA study, cohabiting relationships are also more likely to be plagued with the problems of adultery, alcohol, and drugs. Those who live together prior to marriage are more likely to commit adultery both while living with their partner and if they marry. In addition, one study found that cohabitating women were more jealous than married women, and they had a higher emotional dependency on the male live-in partner. Many developed a pattern of few friendships, no job advancement aspirations, and few outside interests.

Cohabitating couples rate the quality of their relationship much lower than married couples do. Women in these relationships feel less secure economically and emotionally, and they have a much higher rate of depression. Three out of every four cohabitating couples thought their relationship was in serious trouble.

Why does living together apart from marriage set a relationship up for failure? Several studies suggest that those who refuse to make a step of commitment as expressed in marriage do so because they are very individualistic. This is a nice way of saying they are selfish. Those who cohabitated are less likely to express personal character traits that foster a good relationship: sacrifice, humility, flexibility, empathy, and the ability to delay gratification. In the thirty years we have worked with couples, we have seen that those who cohabitate usually also have unhealthy priorities, such as living together so they can have a huge, fancy wedding several years later.

Finally, those who cohabitate prior to marriage are more likely to be discontent or have problems in their sex life. This is a drawback few people talk about, but we have seen it over and over. Trust is the most important factor a woman needs to experience sexual fulfillment, and trust is broken rather than built in a live-in relationship.

If you are intent on being in a relationship, marriage is much more than a piece of paper—it is a ticket to a happier, more fulfilling life together. You might take flak for it, but if you hold tight to your values, you can create an epic love.

Sean and Kimi know firsthand how to paddle upstream in a world that screams, "Try out sex or you'll be sorry!" They discovered by *not* trying out sex that they got the sexual life they had hoped for in marriage. As they share their story, make note of the statements you agree with.

Q: Why did you choose not to have sex or live together before marriage?

Sean and Kimi: We believe the Bible talks clearly about reserving sexual activity for marriage. While in certain social scenes it is unheard of, we sought out people who supported our decisions.

Sean: My parents instilled in me early that sex and living together were best saved for marriage.

Kimi: For me, however, I saw how premarital sex can really hurt girls emotionally. Watching a number of my friends carry that pain into their marriages convinced me it wasn't worth it.

Q: What responses did you get from people when they found out you were *not* sleeping together or living together?

Sean: A few coworkers didn't understand. They assumed we were having sex because we were dating. When they found out we weren't, they wondered why. When I explained that we were waiting till we were married, they couldn't believe it, but they said, "Good for you." It was a strange confirmation of my decision.

Kimi: Usually people were shocked and would say sarcastically, "Seriously?" The interested ones would follow up with, "How is that possible?" or "Why?" or "Oh, that's cute." I was treated differently by my friends at school. Once they found out I didn't have sex, they assumed I was a goody-goody and naïve. Anytime the topic of sex came up, they would look at me as if to say, *You poor thing. You have no idea what we're talking about.* It seemed like they even stopped having conversations when I came around. It was interesting that they felt bad for me and often said there was so much I was missing out on. A few of them had respect for me, though, as they admitted I was doing something they thought they could never do.

Q: How do you feel about your choice to wait until marriage now that you are married?

Sean and Kimi: We both feel it was absolutely the right decision. We get to enjoy each other without the bad effects that we could have brought to our marriage from the past. There is no jealousy or comparison there. It made our honeymoon special, comfortable, and secure knowing that we will be with each other forever physically, emotionally, mentally, and spiritually.

Sexual Integrity

In a previous chapter, we laid out a "how far will you go?" activity to help you each make a commitment before God to protect your sexual integrity before marriage. However, in today's "try it out before marriage" culture, a couple often needs more information to make wise choices as they move through their relationship levels toward marriage.

Let's shoot straight. To best protect your ability to love one person for a lifetime and be *happy* in that marriage relationship, your personal sexual integrity matters most. For the best chances at the lifetime love that is epic in its energy, enthusiasm, and passion, make these critical decisions:

- I will not have sex (intercourse or oral) before marriage.
- If I have past sexual experiences, I will seek to repent (turn away) from that lifestyle and commit to wholehearted moral purity before marriage and sexual faithfulness to my marital partner after marriage.
- I will not live together (cohabitate) before marriage.

The biggest lie Satan has going is that sex is "no big deal." But it is. Sex is God's gift to join two people at the most intimate level: body, soul, and spirit. It's like dynamite. It can cause great gain and carry immense love or great destruction and devastation. Doctors Joe McIlhaney and Freda McKissic Bush have written a book on how the brain works called *Hooked*. The good doctors describe sex as "any intimate contact between two individuals that involves arousal, stimulation, and/or a response by at least one of the two partners." [10] Basically, intimate contact at some point shifts to acquiring the purpose and intention of sexual intercourse.

What Science Has to Say

There is a reason why sexual integrity is so difficult. Here is the science of sex: "This fascinating process is clearly visible with modern brain scan technology, revealing different areas of the brain lighting up." [11] In addition, there is a dopamine addiction that happens when something makes you "feel good." The doctors explain, "When we do something exciting, dopamine rewards us by flooding our brains and making the brain cells produce a feeling of excitement or of well-being…It makes us feel the need or desire to repeat pleasurable, exciting, and rewarding acts. It should be noted, however, that dopamine is values-neutral. In other words, it is an involuntary response that cannot tell right from wrong." [12] Sex is one of the strongest generators of dopamine, so people are "vulnerable to falling into a cycle of dopamine reward for unwise sexual behavior—they can get hooked on it." [13]

In addition, in the female brain, oxytocin, another neurochemical that creates bonding, is also kicked off in sex. It becomes like superglue, but again it is values-neutral. This bonding chemical accumulates so that a person is drawn to stay with another person because of their sexual relationship even if that person is seen as undesirable in other areas—even if they might be abusive or possessive or otherwise dysfunctional. Oxytocin can cause a person to feel their sexual partner is trustworthy—even if he or she is not!

But not just women can experience this irrational bonding through sex. Vasopressin in men creates a similar bonding experience. This bonding is created by God to enhance marital stability, but for singles it can cause a person to attach to someone who might not be healthy for them. If a person decides they do not want to attach to the same partner over and over, but they are addicted to the rush that dopamine creates, they might go from partner to partner. When this action is repeated, it can "cause his or her brain to mold and gel so that it eventually begins to accept this sexual pattern as normal…The pattern of changing sex partners therefore seems to damage their ability to bond in a committed relationship." [14]

Sex Is Hot, Disease Is Not

More than seventy million Americans are living with a sexually transmitted disease. About nineteen million more are diagnosed every year, and the majority are under age twenty-five. [15] "Today there are more than twenty-five sexually transmitted infections worthy of serious concern. Most of these diseases are viral, and though there are drugs to suppress some of them, none of the viral ones can be cured." [16] One in every four teens is infected. [17] "The rates of many STDs, including gonorrhea, genital herpes, and human papillomavirus (HPV), continue to rise rapidly. In addition, the viral chlamydia trachomatis is connected to pelvic inflammatory disease, which is the fastest growing cause of infertility. STDs, in fact, are a direct cause of infertility in both men and women, and an estimated 95 percent of cervical cancer cases are associated with HPV." [18]

One of the most heart-breaking moments of my (Pam's) ministry occurred when I was speaking at an event for mothers. One mom with several small children came up to me after my "red-hot monogamy" talk aimed at married women. In tears she cried,

> My marriage isn't red-hot. It can't be because before I married, I slept with someone other than my husband and he gave me herpes. Now my entire married life is impacted because a person from my past dictates when I can be with my husband. Every outbreak reminds me of my mistake. Every outbreak reminds me that I gave my heart and my body to someone who in turn gave me a disease. Apart from a miracle of science, I will never get rid of this anchor around my marriage.

It Sounds Like Logic

So perhaps you are thinking, *Well then, I won't sleep around. I'll just sleep with the person I am with and we can move in together until we decide to marry. Marriage is just a piece of paper, right?* This might seem like a good line of reasoning except for some compelling arguments why living together is counterproductive to long-term love:

- You are deciding together to disobey God. This is not a great start or a strong foundation to build on.

- You are deciding to not decide on the key issue that moves your future forward. Are you willing to place all your eggs in this relationship basket, knowing that your partner could move to another city, move to another partner, move to another residence at a moment's notice and there is little recourse available to you. Cohabitation by its definition is unstable and insecure, so your life can change overnight.

- You are not actually trying out the relationship because it is not the same as marriage. Living with a back door open, an escape hatch, an exit plan, is not the same as a committed marriage.

 Love Chat

- Are we marrying in the "prime time range"? If not, what extra steps do we need to take to better equip our love to last?

- Do we need to make any changes in how we are navigating our sexual-integrity choices?

- What can we do to best protect our future sexual fulfillment?

- Do we need to ask for help from a clergy member or Christian counselor or help repair any damage we might have caused in our relationship by past choices?

- Have we had all medical tests completed and shared results with each other so we have full disclosure of our sexual history?

Cultures Collide

Our media-enriched world has shrunk. Where it used to be unusual to marry someone from halfway around the globe, it is now commonly accepted. Your grandfather might have married a bride from Germany, Korea, or another country because he was stationed abroad in the military. Today, connections through education, corporations, government agencies, Christian missions, as well as the military, will send singles to far away countries where they may meet and potentially marry someone from a very different culture.

While this sounds exotic and exciting, an interglobal marriage needs to be entered into with caution. Travel to your home country may be covered now by your corporation or the military, so home doesn't feel far away. You can make arrangements to attend major life events such as weddings, funerals, and vacations with family. But at some time in the future, you will be responsible for these costs. It is important to consider how you might feel when buying a ticket home becomes a financial burden rather than an affordable perk. How would you feel if you were not able to be there for a sibling's wedding or a parent's or friend's funeral? It could be a reality.

Given the volatile state of war and terrorism today, what if an enemy suddenly invaded the country you live in and you were separated from your family for the duration of the crisis? How would this make you feel? Would you blame your spouse or face the challenge together? Serious questions must be asked and answered when exploring a cross-cultural marriage. Here are a few to ponder if you are considering tying the knot between two cultures, especially if your extended families live in separate countries.

- Have you both lived at least six months in each other's nation?

- Do you both speak and understand each other's language (or a common language) well enough to have a disagreement and come to a solution that leaves you closer to each other emotionally?

- Do you value and appreciate the cultural traditions on each side?

- Do you have a plan for how to decide what country you will live in immediately after marriage—and later in your marriage?

- Have you consulted a lawyer to fully comprehend any citizenship issues? Any marriage requirements? Prenuptial agreements?

- Do the cultural differences bring up any other differences, such as religion, the treatment of women, how your children will be raised, and so on? How will you handle these additional differences?

- Do you have access to sufficient finances to get both families to the wedding?

- Do you as a couple have the money to get either of you back to your family in case of an emergency or special event?

- Are there family expectations associated with marriage (for example, a period of engagement; a ceremony of approaching parents or grandparents with your intent to marry; the parents living with the newlyweds!). Know what you are getting into.

We have seen cross-cultural marriages work well when a plan is in place to keep the value and appreciation of each culture represented in the marriage. We have also seen couples grow disillusioned because they failed to fully comprehend what it means to live apart from one of their families for years at a time.

Surprise, Surprise

One couple, both Christian leaders, thought they had what it took to make it as a cross-cultural couple. They met in a master's program abroad, so he lived in her country for several years and became comfortable there. After marriage they decided they wanted their children to have the experience of living in both countries. For the first five years, they lived in her country. Then they moved to his home country. A few years into this, he walked in from work one evening to find that his wife had left with their children and gone home to her country. She refused marriage counseling and spent the next decade engaged in a child-custody battle. What started out as a romantic movie script changed into a disaster film that revealed damage at every turn.

Another couple we know fell in love while they were both serving on a mission in a foreign country (neither of their countries of origin). They laid out a plan to live and minister in all three countries over the course of their marriage. They were also diligent to put money aside each year for trips back home, so neither felt deprived of relationships with those they loved. In addition, they created opportunities for their friends and family to come visit them. They had a nice guest room and saved frequent flier miles so those closest to them could fully experience their life and share memories. Each became fluent in the other's language, and they raised their children with a sense of adventure. Travel in various countries was a natural part of their family life.

Love Can Be Colorful

Sometimes cross-cultural relationships blossom among people in the same nation. Just as with overseas connections, this type of marriage merges two distinct family cultures. While the Bible is clear there is only *one* race (the human race), it is equally clear there are many cultures. Some communities will hardly take notice of a biracial marriage while others will view it as a scandal. A couple will be wise to think through how they will handle any prejudices, comments, or even hate crimes should they arise. If you have a unified plan of action, it will be easier to maintain unity if you or your future children encounter negative reactions from friends, family, or even strangers. One biracial couple we know found life easier in larger cities where they were not the *only* colorful couple in the town. They also found some churches were more accepting of their biracial love. In one city, they selected a church because the pastor and his wife were also biracial.

Even if there are negative reactions, if you are a bicultural or biracial couple, here are some questions to discuss so that you each feel valued and loved for who you are:

- How will we evaluate traditions and cultural nuances and decide which to integrate into our marriage and family?
- What will we say or do if we experience any negative blowback from being an intercultural or biracial couple?
- Who do we look to as a healthy role model in dealing with this area of differences?
- If culture differences do become an issue between us, how will we compromise or maintain unity in those areas?
- How can we create a new family that reflects the best of each culture?

DATE *to* DISCOVER

Set a time aside to share your insight into these questions:

- Do either of us have any precious love stories in our family tree?
- How long have couples in each of our families been married?
- Who of our living relatives has been married the longest?

See if you can double-date with a couple you highly respect, either in your family or in your circle of contacts. Offer to take them out to dinner and let them know you want to ask them some questions about love and marriage. Over dinner, ask them:

- Tell us how you met.
- How did you know he/she was "the one"?
- What did you do when dating that you think gave you a great marriage later?

- Do you have any advice on how far one should go physically before marriage?

- Do you have any romantic rituals, nice things you do with and for each other every day to keep your home happy?

- Tell us about your love story, your wedding, and your honeymoon. What was the best choice you made when you were young that you think has paid off now that you are older?

A Little Adam *&* Eve Humor

Whenever your kids are out of control, you can take comfort from the thought that even God's omnipotence did not extend to his kids. After creating heaven and earth, God created Adam and Eve. And the first thing God said to them was: "Don't."

"Don't what?" Adam asked.

"Don't eat the forbidden fruit," said God.

"Forbidden fruit? Really? Where is it?" Adam and Eve asked, jumping up and down excitedly.

"It's over there," said God, wondering why he hadn't stopped after making the elephants.

A few minutes later God saw the kids having an apple break, and he was very angry.

"Didn't I tell you not to eat that fruit?" the First Parent asked.

"Uh-huh," Adam replied.

"Then why *did* you do it?" God asked exasperatedly.

"I dunno," Adam answered.

God's punishment was that Adam and Eve should have children of their own.

6

How Is Our Emotional Fitness?

Coordinate Money and Manage Conflict

May you be poor in misfortune,
Rich in blessings,
Slow to make enemies,
And quick to make friends. [1]

$\mathcal{W}$e all start out immature when it comes to money, and we must determine if we are ready to cooperate on a financial plan in an intimate relationship before saying, "I do."

A young college coed came running in tears to her father. "Dad, you gave me some terrible financial advice!"

"I did? What did I tell you?" said the dad.

"You told me to put my money in that big bank, and now that big bank is in trouble."

"What are you talking about? That's one of the largest banks in the state," he said. "There must be some mistake."

"I don't think so," she sniffed. "They just returned one of my checks with a note saying, 'Insufficient Funds.'" [2]

Obviously, this coed is not quite ready to handle money as an adult. Her reaction is a good reminder to all of us that financial responsibility takes training and maturity. In marriage, it becomes a sensitive issue because everything your partner does affects you emotionally. You have little interest in how others handle their money, but you will have intense interest in the way your life partner earns, saves, and spends money. If you like the way your lover handles money, you will be proud of them and relaxed in your discussions. If you dislike the way they approach finances, you will consistently fight against being angry and disappointed. It makes sense, then, that you would explore financial management before you commit to a lifetime together.

Your Biblical Priorities

The Bible has a lot to say about money. Dave Ramsey, founder of *Financial Peace University,* points out that "money is mentioned in the Bible over 800 times."[3] To put this in perspective, the word *salvation* appears a little over 100 times and *heaven* appears a little over 400 times. In other words, finances are a major theme in the Word of God.

Ask any married couple and they will tell you that money is one of the issues that raises more tension and insecurity than just about anything else. When it comes time to discuss money decisions that will have a pervasive influence on your lives, it is helpful to have God's point of view to rely on. You probably have different opinions than the person you love has on some issues based on the family you grew up in and your preferred approach to life. At times, these opinions are going to collide.

 *Love Chat*

To help you determine your biblical priorities when it comes to money, look over the verses below and identify the four that are most important to you. Then compare your choices with those of your partner.

Rank	Verse	
	1 Timothy 6:6-10	But godliness with contentment is great gain. For we brought nothing into the world, and we can take nothing out of it. But if we have food and clothing, we will be content with that. Those who want to get rich fall into temptation and a trap and into many foolish and harmful desires that plunge people into ruin and

	destruction. For the love of money is a root of all kinds of evil. Some people, eager for money, have wandered from the faith and pierced themselves with many griefs.
Romans 13:6-8	This is also why you pay taxes, for the authorities are God's servants, who give their full time to governing. Give to everyone what you owe them: If you owe taxes, pay taxes; if revenue, then revenue; if respect, then respect; if honor, then honor. Let no debt remain outstanding, except the continuing debt to love one another, for whoever loves others has fulfilled the law.
Proverbs 22:7	The rich rule over the poor, and the borrower is slave to the lender.
Proverbs 15:6	The house of the righteous contains great treasure, but the income of the wicked brings ruin.
Matthew 6:19-21	"Do not store up for yourselves treasures on earth, where moths and vermin destroy, and where thieves break in and steal. But store up for yourselves treasures in heaven, where moths and vermin do not destroy, and where thieves do not break in and steal. For where your treasure is, there your heart will be also."
Matthew 6:25-34	"Therefore I tell you, do not worry about your life, what you will eat or drink; or about your body, what you will wear. Is not life more than food, and the body more than clothes? Look at the birds of the air; they do not sow or reap or store away in barns, and yet your heavenly Father feeds them. Are you not much more valuable than they? Can any one of you by worrying add a single hour to your life? "And why do you worry about clothes? See how the flowers of the field grow. They do not labor or spin. Yet I tell you that not even Solomon in all his splendor was dressed like one of these. If that is how God

		clothes the grass of the field, which is here today and tomorrow is thrown into the fire, will he not much more clothe you—you of little faith? So do not worry, saying, 'What shall we eat?' or 'What shall we drink?' or 'What shall we wear?' For the pagans run after all these things, and your heavenly Father knows that you need them. But seek first his kingdom and his righteousness, and all these things will be given to you as well. Therefore do not worry about tomorrow, for tomorrow will worry about itself. Each day has enough trouble of its own."
	Matthew 6:2-4	"So when you give to the needy, do not announce it with trumpets, as the hypocrites do in the synagogues and on the streets, to be honored by others. Truly I tell you, they have received their reward in full. But when you give to the needy, do not let your left hand know what your right hand is doing, so that your giving may be in secret. Then your Father, who sees what is done in secret, will reward you."
	1 Timothy 5:3-4,8	Give proper recognition to those widows who are really in need. But if a widow has children or grand-children, these should learn first of all to put their religion into practice by caring for their own family and so repaying their parents and grandparents, for this is pleasing to God…Anyone who does not provide for their relatives, and especially for their own household, has denied the faith and is worse than an unbeliever.
	Proverbs 13:11	Dishonest money dwindles away, but whoever gathers money little by little makes it grow.
	Proverbs 21:20-21	The wise store up choice food and olive oil, but fools gulp theirs down. Whoever pursues righteousness and love finds life, prosperity and honor.

| Proverbs 6:6-11 | Go to the ant, you sluggard; consider its ways and be wise! It has no commander, no overseer or ruler, yet it stores its provisions in summer and gathers its food at harvest. How long will you lie there, you sluggard? When will you get up from your sleep? A little sleep, a little slumber, a little folding of the hands to rest—and poverty will come on you like a thief and scarcity like an armed man. |

Your Financial Style

Most people think that if you just have more money, you will have fewer disagreements over money, but that is not necessarily true. Deepseated differences arise because people spend money according to their individual motivation styles.

All of us want to have the possessions that are important to us. As two individuals head toward marriage, the man might think a new truck is a must-have while his girlfriend may think paying off his school bill is extremely important. She might think a $200 handbag on sale for 25 percent off is a steal that he might view as a complete waste of money. You may agree on the importance of funding your dream. If after you are married you have enough money flowing into your budget, you both will be happy. If, however, your budget is limited so that you have to choose a truck or the school bill or put off funding the dream, you will experience conflict. For this reason, a budget is also an expression of your personality and motivation style.

Take a date night this week and talk about which of the following financial motivation styles you each have and brainstorm ways to meet both needs when you establish your future family budget.

Inner Drive 1: Authority

For those who are motivated by having authority (see the discussion in chapter 3 on the Knight in Shining Armor or Queen of Hearts), money is power. It represents options and opportunity. As a result, those with this motivation style are very active with their money. They spend money on whatever goals they consider worthwhile. They invent a plan and take calculated risks to see that plan become a reality.

They are exciting to be around because they are highly productive, visionary, focused, and fearless. They are hardworking, hard-driving people who have the capacity to handle large budgets and large challenges. With spiritual depth and maturity, they can accomplish much for a marriage, a family, a community, or a church. They have a hard time allowing financial opportunities to slip by, so someone motivated by authority usually has a lot of money or they're completely broke!

The temptation for those motivated by authority is to become power-hungry workaholics. The pursuit can become so important that people slip down their priority list. They tell the people in their life that all this hard work is for them, but the relationships can remain elusive because the pursuit of power and wealth is like an aphrodisiac to this person's soul.

If you marry a Knight in Shining Armor or a Queen of Hearts, one compromise might be to set aside a certain amount each month to save toward the big dreamer's long-term goal while a stable amount is reserved for regular family needs. In this way, the visionary makes headway on his or her dream, but the family's bread and butter is not at risk.

Inner Drive 2: Attention

For those who are motivated by attention (Hopeless Romantic), money makes memories. Money is all about people and is a tool in this person's hands to create connections. The heartfelt question that gets asked over and over is, *How will my girlfriend/boyfriend, friends, parents, siblings, coworkers feel when I give them money or spend money on them?*

The shortcoming is that those motivated by attention like to appear as if they have a lot of money—whether they do or not. They love to pick up the tab, throw the lavish party, dress in the latest fashion, or drive the newest, coolest car. They love to spring for fun trips, shopping, or a day of recreation. They are very generous; they will give you the last crumb off the table and the shirt off their back.

If you marry a Hopeless Romantic, your family finances will work out easier if your spouse is given the freedom to work hard to earn extra money that is set aside as discretionary funds to do with as they see fit to enhance relationships. If, however, you handcuff your spouse too much and take away their ability to "bless" the people they love most, they can develop a dramatic edge and become hard to live with. Even in the engagement phase of your relationship, as you begin planning for your future, you might avoid a few arguments if your Hopeless Romantic retains some discretionary funds to build into their relationships.

If you are a Hopeless Romantic, the solution to the ever-pressing inner need to spend money to gain fun or friendship is to picture your most important relationships at the point of every purchase. When you are ready to make a financial decision, picture your partner's face and ask, *Will spending this money please them? Will it help them trust me more?* If you choose to marry the generous heart, create a line-item discretionary amount he or she can spend without consulting you.

Inner Drive 3: Acceptance

The person who is motivated by admiration and acceptance (Wind Beneath My Wings) seeks to purchase peace. The goal is to create as simple a process toward money or resources as possible. When the money is there, they are very cooperative. If finances are tight, they get stubborn because they believe a crisis is being created that will disrupt the peace in their lives. At this point, they will either work harder, argue, or dig their heels in to find a path out of the crisis.

If the couple or family is spending less than this person makes, he or she relaxes. If the couple or family is spending more than this person makes, he or she will grow to resent the spending habits of their mate and family because they feel appreciated only as the provider of a paycheck rather than as a person.

If you marry someone characterized by the inner drive of *acceptance*, they have a remarkable ability to simplify things when it comes to finances. They remind us that life is not all about money. They are peacemakers and natural mediators, so they are good at problem solving financial issues whenever those issues cause harm.

You will find that your future marriage is better when as a couple you commit to a savings account because it helps the person with this motivational style relax. As long as there is money in the bank to cover contingencies, this person can be at peace. As long as there is a simple way to stay ahead, they will be very cooperative and more willing to go with the flow of the family's spending needs.

Inner Drive 4: Accuracy

The accurate person (True Blue Lover) is all about a system, and they are emotionally attached to the process. When a budget is set, they interpret the figures literally. So if the budget says fifty dollars for groceries per week, it means fifty dollars—not fifty-five and not sixty. The budget is a mandate they live by. However, because they love managing money and resources, they often have money and resources to manage. They are savers, planners, and investors (as long as the investment is prudent and safe). They spend money according to a cautious, practical, and wise long-range plan. This is the spouse that may say "I love you" with snow tires because you need them to keep you safe.

Because they are so inflexible and rigid about the plan, they can often miss great financial opportunities. This person will make sure the family is never without money, but cooperating with the budget might be a challenge for your personality. The key to working things out is to discuss ahead of time any foreseen changes or adaptations that might need to occur. Accuracy motivated people are precise but they are generally reasonable, so if you give good reasons, you will get cooperation.

This person also needs consistent encouragement, so if you marry someone motivated by *accuracy*, daily expressions of appreciation will go a long way in keeping the cooperation level high in your marriage— and helping them stay positive and open to financial ideas you might express. Say "thank you" often. This will be easier to do if you remember that it is less likely you will get into financial binds because True Blue Lover takes pride in being savvy financially.

As you can see, some motivation styles put more emphasis on spending while others focus more on saving—and often opposites do attract! If either of these emphases is out of control, the spender may accumulate heavy debt while the saver avoids legitimate opportunities because of fear. These are not good ingredients for a cooperative marriage and will create emotional turmoil for you as a couple if not addressed effectively. So, before you convince yourself that money is not going to be an issue, ask yourself, *Am I (or the person I am dating) putting an unhealthy emphasis on either spending or saving?*

If as a couple you discuss and then budget in a way that includes your motivations, there will be fewer arguments. For example, Pam is Inner Drive 2, and making memories with family and friends is what makes life worth living. She is willing to work hard to create these memories, so we have a line item in our budget to give her freedom to make a few memories. Bill is Inner Drive 3, so Pam has agreed to ways of money management that make Bill's life a little easier when it comes to monthly bills.

No money motivation style is right or wrong as long as you keep in mind biblical mandates of respect, honor, love, and desire to create a spirit of unity by valuing the way God wired your mate.

To keep money from becoming a consistent negative issue after you are married, you might want to read one of the books on personal finances by Ellie Kay, Ron Blue, Larry Burkett, or Dave Ramsey. We recommend that all those considering marriage not tie the knot until they complete a program like Dave Ramsey's *Financial Peace University* or Crown Financial Ministries' *MoneyLife Personal Finance Study.*

 Love Chat

To help you get a snapshot of what your motivational combination looks like, each of you fill in the following chart.

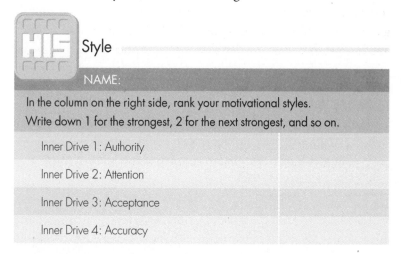

Style

NAME:

In the column on the right side, rank your motivational styles.
Write down 1 for the strongest, 2 for the next strongest, and so on.

Inner Drive 1: Authority

Inner Drive 2: Attention

Inner Drive 3: Acceptance

Inner Drive 4: Accuracy

Style

In the column on the right side, rank your motivational styles.
Write down 1 for the strongest, 2 for the next strongest, and so on.

Inner Drive 1: Authority

Inner Drive 2: Attention

Inner Drive 3: Acceptance

Inner Drive 4: Accuracy

- What possible disagreements do you foresee?
- Can you picture how to dovetail your styles?
- Can you each succeed if coupled with your loved one's style?

Men and Women Spend Differently

In our modern world, we are hesitant to say that men and women approach life differently, but studies indicate that in the area of money, some significant differences exist. Journalist Natalie McNeal compiled much of this research for buzzfeed.com and found ten ways the genders differ in the way they spend money. Here's a summary of her findings:

1. Women spend more on clothes; men spend more on food. Almost 64 percent of women admit to shopping for clothes, food, and shoes to lighten their mood. Men shop mostly for food, electronics, and music or movies when they want a pick-me-up.

2. Women give more to charity. In a 2010 Center on Philanthropy report, researchers found that women give more money to charity than men in practically every income group.

3. Boys spend more on booze. Single men spent an annual average of $507 on alcohol, says the Bureau of Labor Statistics 2010-2011 annual report. The single ladies? A mere $216.

4. Single ladies win at spending to look right. Single women spend an average of $524 per year on personal care and services; men only $194.

5. Men spend the most on Valentine's Day. Nearly two-thirds of men purchase flowers for Valentine's Day. Only one-third of women buy them. Men spend almost double what women spend on the holiday.

6. Men save more for retirement. One survey found that men have 28.8 percent more ($50,632) in their 401(k)s than women ($39,320). Also, men have a 72 percent higher balance in their IRAs.

7. Men spend more when women are scarce. Men spend more money when they think there are fewer women around. Also, researchers found that single men have higher debt and more credit cards in cities where the gender ratios show fewer women.

8. Women are more patient for online deals. Women take 40 percent longer to make a purchase and are more likely to do price-comparison shopping than men.

9. Men spend more on nightlife (but not much). The average single man spends $1,545 a year on entertainment, and women almost match that at $1,432.

10. Women may be better at paying back loans. Micro-creditors have found that "women not only repay loans more often than men, but that when women control the money, their families were more likely to benefit from the income," according to the *Wall Street Journal*. [4]

 Love Chat

Look over the list of differences in the way men and women spend money and discuss the following questions with each other:

- Which of the ten ways are true about us as a couple?
- Which of the ten ways are not true about us as a couple?
- Do any of the ten ways appear to be an area of conflict for us? If so, why?

The Heart of Work

Early in your relationship, you can afford to focus on your love for each other, concluding that you can face any challenge because of your devotion. As time passes, you are going to realize that life is going to cost you a small fortune. You must work and you must work hard in order to support an adult life and provide for a family. It is common for this part of life to become a significant point of contention. First, because the financial demands of life are real. Second, because we aren't very skilled at balancing our desire to be successful with our desire to be intimately connected.

You may be attracted to your partner today because of a strong work ethic and the dedication she brings to financial productivity. In time, this same dedication can make you feel neglected, as if you are less important than work. Or you may love being with your partner today because of the relaxed environment he brings to your relationship. In time, this same laid-back approach can be a significant source of irritation when there isn't enough money to keep up with your bills.

It is important, therefore, that you explore your financial potential as a couple before you decide that love is all it takes. You don't necessarily need to be making enough money today to provide for an active family, but you do need to be confident you have the potential.

We were married at twenty years old and barely had enough money to survive. We lived in a modest apartment, had about half as much furniture as we needed, rode bikes to save on gas, and almost never ate out. Our combined salaries in those early years were sorely deficient to provide for children, but we knew we had the work ethic and the goals to get there. We had this confidence because we saw the evidence in other areas. We were both dedicated athletes as teenagers. We worked hard to get good grades. We actively served in a campus ministry for about ten hours each week in addition to school and work.

In determining your financial potential as a couple, you will want to explore your work goals and your work ethic. The exercises below will help you explore these issues together. Take time to fill in the information and then discuss your answers with each other.

Work Goals

Anyone who has succeeded in a career began with a target in mind. It could be a goal of how much money you want to earn, a position you want to achieve, or a certain outcome you want to experience. It is common to adjust the goals as you go because none of us can see into the future, but the process of having goals keeps us in motion so we can discover the dream God has placed in our hearts. Someone who has goals today, no matter how small, will likely be successful in the future. Discuss the following questions with your partner to determine if goal-setting is active:

- What is my overall goal for my career or education?
- What step do I want to take toward this goal in the coming year?
- What career steps do I want to take in the next five years?
- How do these steps match my pace in life? Will it speed up life or slow it down? If so, for how long?

Work Ethic

Each of us has a certain level of interest in work. You may gain great satisfaction from the work you perform or you may see it as a necessary means to provide a living. You will do well to identify your intensity level so you can coordinate your careers with this in mind. As responsibilities in life grow, you will make decisions that allow you to operate at your preferred level of commitment to work. Fill in the two worksheets below and then discuss them with your partner.

Prioritize each aspect of your career listed below by circling the appropriate letter (with *A* representing a high priority, *B* a moderate priority, and *C* a low priority). Use a different color ink for each of you.

A	B	C	I want to work full-time for a company.
A	B	C	I want to work for a company but telecommute from a home office.
A	B	C	I want to work part-time.
A	B	C	I want a regulated schedule.
A	B	C	I want to own my own business.
A	B	C	I want a steady paycheck.
A	B	C	I want freedom to determine my schedule.
A	B	C	I want to work in order to have health insurance.
A	B	C	I want to work hard on my career when our kids are young.
A	B	C	I want to work hard on my career when our kids are teenagers.
A	B	C	I want to work hard on my career after our kids leave home.
A	B	C	I want to retire early.
A	B	C	I never want to retire (possibly change careers or downscale hours, but I love working).

Evidence Collection:
Mark the statement that best describes your desire to pursue a career.

Him	Her	
❏	❏	I dream about being as effective as possible in my career.
❏	❏	I value my family more when they value my career.
❏	❏	I feel good about my life when I am working hard.
❏	❏	I like going to work about as much as I like being home.

☐	☐	I like to go to work, but I could give it up.
☐	☐	I like my time at home better than my time at work.
☐	☐	I like life best when I don't have to work.
☐	☐	I gain much more satisfaction in life from volunteer activities than I do from work.

God First

The bottom line of all finances is stewardship. God is the owner of everything, and he is directing everything toward the accomplishment of his will. To this end, he has entrusted each of us with a number of resources. These resources are not actually ours; we must leave them behind when our days on earth are ended. They have, however, been put in our care during our earthly stay.

To help us keep a clear focus on the stewardship of finances, we have been instructed to give the first part of our income back to God. Many people seem to view this pragmatically—God must need money so we have to give so he will have something to spend.

Our giving, however, has nothing to do with God's needs. It is all about directing our hearts. Jesus was very clear that our hearts are connected to our money. His primary instruction about money is found in Luke 12:34, "For where your treasure is, there your heart will be also." Whatever we spend money on, we fall in love with! If we spend money on God first, we will be connected to him and will be motivated to pursue a vibrant, active relationship with him.

 Love Chat

What percentage of your income would you like to give back to God?

10 percent
25 percent
5 percent
90 percent and live on 10 percent
Something else

Briefly write down why you want to give this amount.

Make an appointment with your partner to discuss your preference and the reasons behind it.

Your Golden List

Once you are married, you will want to write down your financial plan and keep track of both income and expenses. We suggest you discuss together prior to marriage the following list, which includes budgetary priorities for each of the motivation styles. It is our experience that a couple cooperates with the budget better when a part of it includes the foundational motivation builders in each person's life.

We realize that you will have to speculate on the dollar amounts for many of the items in this sample budget. Simply make an educated guess for those items you are unsure of. You might even ask your parents or other married couples you know well for the amounts they would suggest based on their experience. Think of this initial attempt at a budget as a first draft, not the final document. Use the blank lines to personalize your expenditures.

Once you are married, you will want to keep a copy of your budget in your bill file, save it in a strategic place on your computer, or keep it with your checkbook as a reminder of the agreements you have made together.

Evidence Collection:

OUR MOTIVATIONAL BUDGET			
Assign To	Description	Monthly	Yearly
❏ H ❏ W	Income		
	His salary		
	Her salary		
	Investment income (itemize)		

	Other income (itemize)		
	Total Income:		
❏ H ❏ W	**Giving to God**		
❏ H ❏ W	**Fixed Expenses**		
	Mortgage (or rent)		
	Property insurance		
	Utilities—gas and electric		
	Utilities—water and trash		
	Utilities—phone and cable		
	Home maintenance and repair		
	Auto expense		
	Car payment		
	Gasoline		
	Insurance		
	Repair and maintenance		
	Life insurance		
	Groceries		
	Toiletries		
	Motivational Priorities		
❏ H ❏ W	**Inner Drive 1: Authority**		
	Investments		
	Risks for our future		

☐ H ☐ W	Inner Drive 2: Attention		
	Entertainment		
	Social events		
	Vacation		
☐ H ☐ W	Inner Drive 3: Acceptance		
	Savings		
	Emergency fund		
☐ H ☐ W	Inner Drive 4: Accuracy		
	Retirement funds		
	College fund (for each child)		
	Total Expenses:		
	Income – Expenses:		

The key to making any budget work is responsibility. After you are married, you must take the responsibility to fill in the list of income and expenses and negotiate your commitments so your income is greater than your expenses. Then you must take personal responsibility for the items that will be assigned to you. We suggest the following steps for making this plan work:

Step 1: Fill out the financial worksheet. When marriage becomes a serious possibility for you (shortly before or immediately after you get engaged), it is wise to prepare a budget you will use after you are married. Each of you bring a copy of your current working budget and simply begin consolidating the numbers. This will begin the process of merging two financial streams into one river. You may consider meeting with a mentor couple, clergy, or counselor to gain their wisdom and advice on your financial plan. If your financial portfolios are contradictory or complicated, seek out a financial advisor, or even a lawyer, to help you address your challenges as early as possible. Take plenty of time to work through the numbers and to decide which of you is best to handle each aspect of your financial world.

It will most likely take more than one meeting to settle all the issues involved, but in the long run, it will be well worth the investment. Remember that this is much more than math. The decisions you will make about your money will help you give expression to your dreams, your motivations, and your hopes. If things get tense, take a break and reschedule your meeting. Just keep rescheduling until you have finished.

Step 2: Take personal responsibility for everything that is assigned to you. Make a copy of your financial worksheet for each of you and empower each other to take responsibility. As you get engaged, you might decide to create an account for wedding expenses. If you will be the one responsible for getting money in the bank, you must be able to make deposits. If you will have responsibility for making payments, you must be able to access an account with checks, debit cards, or credit cards.

Decide how you will manage your money and accounts after your wedding. Will you each have a personal account with another mutual account for household expenses that you contribute to? Will you merge all monies and share all debt and all income in common? Who will pay what bill and when? If you decide ahead of time how money is earned, saved, spent, and accounted for, there will be fewer arguments after your wedding date. The more specific your plan, the more unity you will experience.

Step 3: Meet regularly to coordinate financial activity and make adjustments. You can plan to meet weekly, monthly, or quarterly. The key is to meet consistently and willingly. The goal of this meeting will be to share with each other how your part of the plan is working. It is best if you include plenty of affirmation in each other's areas of strengths. Financial discussions tend to get emotional, so you might as well make the emotional energy work for you! At these meetings, feel free to make adjustments to the financial plan as necessary.

Conflict Is Normal

A discussion about money seems like a good place to add some thoughts about conflict. We get into conflict with each other because we get emotionally stirred up about something and can't keep quiet about it. Since we are all emotional about our money, many of our conflicts start out as financial discussions.

Conflict is an ordinary part of every intimate relationship. We all entertain the thought that we should be able to get along with this person who has captured our hearts because there is something special between us. While this is true most of the time, it is nearly impossible to connect your life to another and not have significant disagreements. As you go through your journey together, you will get under each other's skin and challenge each other to search the depths of your heart for what really matters to you.

Conflict, however, does not need to be destructive if you guide it rather than let it get out of control. One of life's great truths is that our emotions follow our decisions, which is good news when it comes to disagreements. If you decide ahead of time how you will face conflict, you can guide your emotional energy so that it draws you together and adds value to your relationship. Two decisions that will help you direct your conflicts in a positive way are choosing your conflict-resolution style and agreeing on a conflict covenant.

Your Conflict Style

When faced with a conflict in your relationship, choose one of the following approaches.

The Planned Approach

Schedule a time to discuss what you are upset about. Your conflicts will almost always be highly emotional. This person to whom you will say "I do" is the only person on earth you will share everything with—your finances, your emotions, your bodies, your social calendar, and your dreams. As a result, when you have a disagreement, intense emotions surface with the potential to take over the discussion. This is further complicated by the fact that men tend to get flooded by intense emotions and shut down in defense. When this happens, couples often struggle to reach any kind of resolution because their emotions take over the conversation and override their logic. Scheduling a meeting gives you an opportunity to prepare your heart and your thoughts for navigating the discussion.

Before the meeting, describe in writing the issue as you are aware of it. Keep in mind that the presenting issue is not always the real issue, but you have to start somewhere. If you can clearly state your thoughts about the disagreement without reacting to each other, you will have a much better chance of resolving the conflict. At the meeting, proceed along the following steps to SOLVE the issue:

1. Seek God together. Pray together and ask God to give you wisdom to work through the issue.

2. Open the conversation. Decide who is going to share first. There are a number of ways you can manage this. For instance, you can buy a small piece of carpet that you pass back and forth. Whoever has the floor (carpet) will do the talking. The one who does not have the floor will do nothing but listen. When you are done, pass the carpet to your spouse and take your turn listening. You can also choose a small ball that you roll back and forth with the statement, "The ball is in your court." (This one may not be a good idea if you are demonstrative people who are likely to throw the ball at each other!) You can even use a piece of paper that you take turns holding so you can "get on the same page." These are simple tools to help you stay on track while you keep your emotions in check. Keep the dialogue going until you feel the environment soften between the two of you.

3. *Look deeper.* After both of you have shared sufficiently, ask, "What do you think the real issue is?" It may be the issue you have been talking about or it may be something else. It could be a reaction to something from your past or something you are afraid of. It is also possible that stress has risen in your life and you are taking the stress out on each other. It is also possible that you are upset with your partner about the best traits in his or her life.

4. *Verify options.* Once you have identified the real issue, discuss possible solutions. We have found it best to write down the ideas we come up with rather than trust them to memory. If one of the ideas becomes an obvious solution and you can both agree on it, commit to it and begin to implement your agreement. If the solution is not obvious, pray together and then set another meeting to discuss the solution. This will give you a day or two to consider the ideas you came up with. Since emotions rise and fall in their intensity, time will help you think through your solutions when your emotional intensity diminishes.

5. *Evolve into the answer.* Get back together in a day or two to discuss a solution. Be patient at this point. Some challenges in life don't actually have solutions. For example, you may have a special needs child who regularly creates stress in your relationship. You may experience a financial setback that will take years to recover from. You may face a health issue that will force your life to change. You will learn to adjust to these stresses, but you won't actually fix them. You will look for ways to grow together while you live with the challenge, but you won't ever really return to a normal life. As you navigate these challenges together, you will discover a depth in your love that is your reward for taking the journey together. If you practice evolving into an answer when issues are smaller today, you will be better prepared for the larger storms you will encounter in the future.

The Spontaneous Approach

The spontaneous approach for handling conflict takes the most self-control and relational skill. In this approach, you deal with issues as they come up. You don't wait, you don't reschedule, and you don't give yourself time to gather your composure. You just jump in and try to get to the heart of the matter. There are a few skills that will help you in this approach.

Insulate. Use "I" statements instead of "you" statements. It's easy to say you will do this when you are calm, but it is a very different matter when you are upset with each other. "You" statements sound like accusations when they are mixed with negative emotions. "You did this," "You are so inconsiderate," "You were being selfish," may be statements of truth, but they easily elicit defensive responses. Your ability to use "I" statements will determine your ability to successfully work through these discussions. "I was surprised by what happened," "I am very upset by this situation," "I was shocked when this happened and I reacted very strongly," are statements that do not avoid the subject but give the other person an opportunity to respond without getting defensive. If you choose this approach, keep in mind that the statement, "I think you are wrong (or stupid or inconsiderate)," is not an "I" statement!

Investigate. Take time to relieve the pressure by describing what you believe the issue is. The purpose of this phase is to lower the intensity of the emotional climate between the two of you. Ask the question, "What is the real issue we are facing?" As with all conflicts, the goal is to identify the issues that are at the heart of your reaction so you can find a positive direction to move.

Identify. Brainstorm solutions. Verbally investigate possible ways to address the conflict. Take enough time to explore possibilities to see if a new solution surfaces that wasn't clear in the heat of the moment.

Initiate. Commit to a course of action based on your conclusions.

Interconnect. The reason you have such intense discussions with each other is the emotional connection you have. Before you end your discussion, seek to rediscover what it is you love about each other. You are highly attractive to each other, but we believe these attractive traits can also have a dark side that may show itself and create intense negative responses. Since these negative responses are attached to the things you love about the other person, they can easily be turned positive.

This is why "make-up" sex is a common experience for married couples. They are upset with each other, argue through the issue, reach a conclusion, and then rediscover their attraction to each other. That rediscovery is where you want all of your arguments to end so that they work for you rather than tear you apart.

The Delayed Approach

If scheduling a meeting or having a spontaneous discussion do not work for you, you might try taking a short break before you work your way through an issue. The purpose of the break is to calm your emotions and get yourself back to a more rational place. It is more reliable if you choose a specific time to get back together, but you may be able to say, "As soon as we calm down, let's get back together." If you take this approach, you will want to check in with each other every couple of hours to see if you have calmed down. If you do not diligently check in, it is likely you will ignore the issue and conclude that time has taken care of everything. This is like planting a land mine in the middle of your relationship. If you do this enough times, those mines will eventually erupt and cause severe damage. It is much better to deal with the issues as individual discussions rather than waiting for a compound problem to unleash itself.

When you get together, you will want to follow the same steps as above:

- *Insulate.* Use "I" statements instead of "you" statements.
- *Investigate.* Take time to relieve the pressure by asking, "What is the real issue we are facing?"
- *Identify.* Brainstorm solutions.
- *Initiate.* Commit to a course of action based on your conclusions.
- *Interconnect.* Before you end your discussion, seek to discover what it is you love about each that caused this disagreement.

 *Love Chat*

On the chart below, mark which approach to conflict you prefer. Then write a brief description of why you chose this approach. Once you have filled this out, discuss your answers with your partner.

His	Hers	Conflict Style
		Planned Approach
		Spontaneous Approach
		Delayed Approach

I prefer this conflict style for the following reasons:

Him:

Her:

Do we believe we can effectively manage conflict as a couple? Why or why not?

If you are brave, tackle a source of conflict in your relationship and use one of the methods above to seek a solution. Pick an easy issue for the first run. Maybe the solution to world peace, the national deficit, or how to raise the Dow can be put off for another day.

Your Conflict Covenant

In the absence of decisions about how you will approach conflict, you will simply do what you know to do, which is based on what you saw in your parents. If they were healthy in their approach, you are in good shape. If their skills were deficient, it is likely yours will be also.

This was a big issue for us because our parents were out of control when it came to arguing. Both our parents would scream at each other and launch unfair accusations. Bill's mom was a thrower who would launch plates, cups, and food in fits of rage. Pam's dad would yell obscenities and throw tools during moments of alcohol-fueled rage. We were glad our parents were verbal, but the rest of the circus was not something we wanted to repeat.

We decided early in our relationship we needed to make a *conflict covenant* so that our propensity for drama would be held in check. Here are our conflict rules of engagement we set in place for after the "I do":

Check the timing. Is this the best time to talk? If it is personal, emotional, or not for kids' ears, we wait and make it private. If we are tired, we might begin the discussion and reschedule for a time when we are better rested. Did one of us already have a bad day? Then wait.

Check our closeness. If the issue is really important, we go away and spend time together reconnecting first. Then we talk after we are rested, have enjoyed some friendship activities, made love, and so on.

Check our voice tone, body language, and attitude. Am I communicating love with what is unsaid? This has been a huge learning process for me (Pam) as Bill is a very sensitive man and easily wounded by my tone. I think I am being passionate or intense; he interprets it as harsh and judgmental.

One day after he said I had hurt him still again, I responded, "Then teach me. Teach me how you want me to express myself in a way that I can release my feelings and give you the needed input, but in a way that doesn't wound you. Bill, I love you. I don't want to wound you every time we have an issue we have to talk through. Teach me what I can do differently or what words would be a better choice to use." And he did. He'd say, "When you say *you should...you need to...you ought to...*I feel disrespected." Then when I'd raise my voice or get a certain inflection, he'd stop me and say, "Pam, when you say it in that tone of voice, it shuts me down emotionally."

This was a hard decision for me to make in allowing Bill to redesign how I communicate, but I believe it saved our marriage. I believe it paid big dividends later when I became a parent. My sons and I now enjoy great communication at a deep level because we all have learned a more healthy way to express our feelings in a way others can listen and receive. I had to put my pride aside for the greater good and the greater goal of love.

Check in with God. We begin and end and sometimes stop in the middle to pray. If the argument is going down a destructive path and we recognize we are hurting each other, we will often stop in the middle and pray. Sometimes we have to stop, pray, and take a break for a few days. We use this time to check into God's Word, think about the situation, and process our own emotions.

Check negative actions at the door. We have banned certain words and behaviors from our interaction. Our list includes words we won't say to each other, including, "I want a divorce," "I hate you," "You are stupid," "I think I married the wrong person," and "I'm out of here." They also include actions such as leaving in anger, slamming doors, driving away in a rage. The drama we grew up around made it easy to resort to outlandish behavior, so we chose early on to rule them out before they became habits.

 *Love Chat*

Write a first draft of your conflict covenant. Be as creative as you like or as analytical as you like. The key is to put real decisions on paper on how you will approach each other when you disagree. To help you in the process, you may want to include:

- The conflict style we think we will be most effective with.
- The things we will never say to each other.
- The negative actions we will avoid.
- Habits we have noticed in other couples that seem effective.

Our Conflict Covenant

Money and conflict go a long way in determining how successful you will be as a couple. We are all imperfect, so we will clash with each other at times. We are all attached to our finances, so we will struggle to stay on the same page with our budgets. If you can convince yourself you can handle these two areas of the journey, there is almost nothing else that could ever get between you.

DATE *to* DISCOVER

Take the budget worksheet from this chapter to your favorite coffee shop or bakery. Work on the first draft of your future budget as you share a snack. The casual atmosphere and shared treats will help you relax.

A Little Adam & Eve Humor

Adam was walking around the Garden of Eden feeling very lonely, so God asked him, "What is wrong with you?"

Adam said he didn't have anyone to talk to.

God said, "I was going to give you a companion and it would be a woman. This person will cook for you and wash your clothes. She will always agree with every decision you make. She will bear your children and never ask you to get up in the middle of the night to take care of them. She will not nag you, and will always be the first to admit she was wrong when you've had a disagreement. She will never have a headache, and will freely give you love and compassion whenever needed."

Adam asked God, "What would a woman like this cost me?"

God said, "An arm and a leg."

Adam asked, "What can I get for just a rib?"

How Will You Propose?

Make Your Big Moment a Big Moment

May you see each other through many dark days,
and make all the rest a little brighter. [1]

$\mathcal{W}$e are sure when you "pop the question" you will want to make it count! This will become one of the most important memories in your life, and it deserves some planning and preparation. We encourage you to make your proposal an event that can be passed down as part of your love story from generation to generation.

For the Bride-to-Be

In a lot of ways your proposal is out of your control. The groom-to-be will make most of the choices about how and when you get engaged. This is an exciting time for you, but it can also be stressful because you have opinions about how it ought to go. As a result, we want to talk with you about this big day in your life before we walk the groom-to-be through the process of creating a memorable proposal. You can make a few decisions that will help create a proposal-friendly environment.

Value yourself enough to want a memorable proposal. Men have a tendency to simplify relationships, so they often have not thought ahead about the importance of the actual proposal. If you are willing to forgo being pursued and honored with a well-thought-out proposal, your man will most likely accept that as evidence that it isn't very important.

Don't overdo it, but let him know it is important to you to experience a proposal that adds value to your love.

Value the timing enough to be patient. Many young ladies unintentionally sabotage their relationships around the time their man is going to pop the question. Most men we know like to have some sense of surprise in asking a woman to marry them, so the delay might simply be due to his steps of preparation. What he needs most is your patience, not your panic. As you wait for him, watch out for the stirrings in your heart that tend to make you impatient.

"Is today the day?" Some women wake up every day looking for clues that today might be the big day. As each day passes without a ring, she gets moodier and more sullen.

"What's wrong with you?" Some brides-to-be start doubting their decision. They second-guess their love or their man as his delay is interpreted negatively. Thoughts such as, *he doesn't care, he doesn't love me enough, he must not be all in,* dominate her thinking and inadvertently deteriorate the relationship.

"Step up, buddy!" Other young ladies grow increasingly angry and demanding if the proposal doesn't come in her timing.

"What's wrong with me?" Some girlfriends begin to think they are not worthy or are too imperfect to be asked. Relentless questions about how important she is can overwhelm her boyfriend and erode his interest.

Which doubting design do you fall into? Write a letter to God and discuss your emotions, doubts, and fears.

Value your man enough to pray for him. To battle doubt, you will need to sow faith. One way to grow your faith and love is to develop the habit of praying for your man while you wait. If you want a husband who is a strong leader, pray for his leadership ability and your willingness to follow that kind of leader. Men rely on the strength of their wife, so your ability to believe in and express your confidence in your man will be of critical importance in the days ahead.

To assist you in praying, consider using the words of Proverbs. Read one chapter in Proverbs each day and choose words to form a prayer for your man. After you pray for him, send him a text or an email with a positive message that does not mention your desire for him to propose or buy you a ring. In the years to come, you will be glad you have learned the pattern of praying for and supporting your man. There will be many "waiting rooms" in the years ahead, so become a woman who is proactive in your waiting today. It will bless all your tomorrows.

For the Groom-to-Be

You don't have to be an incredibly innovative person to create a proposal that will linger for a lifetime. The Holy Spirit is willing to give you ideas and guide your decisions. No one knows the one you love better than the God who created her, and he has promised to give you wisdom if you are willing to ask (James 1:5). Once you have prayed, work through the following steps for a romantically strong proposal.

Personalize It

There has never been a relationship exactly like yours. You have special memories and tender ways of interacting that add value to your love. To help you incorporate these into your proposal, ask yourself:

Is there a special day to propose? Is there a day of the week or a date on the calendar that is special to the two of you? We know one family where five generations of couples have married on the same date. Another couple met at a subway stop on a certain date, so he decided to propose at that same station one year later.

Is there a special time of day to propose? Sunrise, sunset, or another time of day may have special interest for you as a couple. If so, plan your proposal to coincide with this time.

Is there a special location where I would like to propose? It there a country, a city, a geographic location that has meaning in your love story? We know a plethora of couples who met at Christian conference centers and camps who returned to those memorable locations to begin their engagement.

What do I want to say when I propose? What is it that you want to communicate besides "Will you marry me?" As you pray through this, be yourself. Don't fill your proposal with words you would never say in any other context, but strive to be your best self at this critical moment. You can search the Internet for "proposal wording" to inspire your own thinking, but in the end your fiancée wants to hear your heart speak.

Here are some guidelines to pull together the best words for the one you love. Use words:

- *From your feelings about her.* Do you cherish her? Love her? Can't picture your life without her?

- *From her world.* If she is an artist, a photographer, a servant of God, an athlete, or a businesswoman, use a word picture that relates to her daily pursuits. For example, you may say to an artist, "I want to bring the colors of our lives together to paint a beautiful painting."

- *From Scripture.* A Bible verse may capture your heart for her or the vision God has laid out for your lives together. Or perhaps God used a verse to raise your confidence to take the step to marry your beloved. If so, share it!

- *She can remember.* This will be a precious moment in her life. The good news is "less is more" when it comes to a proposal. Just a few sentences will be plenty.

Pulling It Together

In the spaces below, write down your thoughts on how you would like to personalize your proposal. Guys, we suggest you ask your girlfriend the first three questions. You may think you already know her answers, but it's a good idea to ask. Also, make note of her sentimental habits or desires. Perhaps she always wants to watch a sunset, or she has said more than once that she loves her grandparents' cabin on the lake, or the waves of the ocean help her relax, or she talks about a significant date in her family.

Questions to Personalize Our Wedding Proposal		
Personalized Question	His Response	Her Response
Are there special dates on the calendar I should consider?		

Is there a special time of day I should consider?		
Are there special locations I should consider?		
Words to consider from:		
The way I feel about her		
Her world		
Scripture		

Don't feel you need to memorize what you are going to say. If you want to share a short love letter, a poem, or a song, read it as part of your proposal. The sincerity in your heart will come through. Be flexible because nerves or the excitement of the moment may cause the words to tumble out or get a little jumbled.

Our daughter-in-law Caleigh said, "I had no idea when Zach asked me to walk to the dock at my papa's lakefront property on Thanksgiving Day that he was going to propose. That was until he gave me a tight hug. His heart was beating so hard and fast I could feel it through both of our winter jackets! Zach told me later that he had prepared a longer speech packed with words of deep meaning. In the end, however, he was so excited he jumped ahead to, 'Caleigh, I love you! Will you please be my wife?'"

Our friend, Holly, has a fun story of how her husband, Mike, personalized his proposal:

> When my husband and I were dating, I once told him if a man was going to propose, he should "go big." So when it came time for Mike to declare his love for me, he really went all out.
>
> I was working as a producer at a TV news station. Without my knowledge, Mike arranged for my coworkers to

help him execute his plan. The day before his proposal, my boss called me in to work the morning shift, to "fill in" for a writer who was sick.

When the 6:00 a.m. news came on, the producer frantically asked me to head to a special desk in the newsroom to find an email our helicopter reporter needed to read on the air. What I didn't know was that our crew had secretly placed a microphone under the keyboard and had a camera trained on that desk.

All of a sudden, I looked at the TV monitor and saw my boyfriend in front of a big white cross on top of a local mountain. The fence around the cross was decorated with two giant white doves, carrying enormous "gold" wedding rings.

As the helicopter pilot filmed Mike from above, the studio camera filmed my reaction on the ground. Our families and friends were watching it all unfold live on their TV screens.

What I loved most about that amazing proposal is that Mike catered to my frugal side. Apart from buying my engagement ring, his elaborate show of love didn't cost him a dime!

Plan It

A memorable proposal often needs some advanced planning. Plan a proposal that matches your organizational skill and personality. If you are an easygoing couple, an elaborate proposal might not be fitting. On the other hand, your skills as a leader, a business owner, or party planner may lend itself to a more elaborate affair.

You can do an Internet search for ideas to inspire you or invest in an app, such as *Proposal Pal, Proposal Pro,* or others, that allows you to plug in answers to key questions to help plan a personalized proposal.

Our friends Matt and Anne are ministry leaders with terrific instincts for administration, and their proposal story reflects it! Anne captured the moment for us:

I was in Paris nannying for an American family. Matt had contacted some new friends of mine over there who were church planters and asked if they would help. He also recruited a friend in the States to send preplanned emails so that I would think he was still back home. Unbeknownst to me, Matt flew to France and showed up at the Eiffel Tower, where I was going with my friends for a birthday party. As we walked onto the second floor, my friends started taking pictures, and Matt came out of nowhere. Needless to say, I was very surprised.

I kept thinking to myself, *Listen! You'll want to remember!* I can't remember everything he said, but I do remember him getting down on one knee and saying "Anne Elaine Savage, will you marry me?" He then took off my promise ring and put on the engagement ring. He hung out for eight more days while I gave him the tour of Paris. I was supposed to stay for one year, but decided after three months and a proposal to come home early!

Matt's financial investment, his honoring Anne's parents by bringing them in on the plan, his relationship building with Anne's friends in France, and his ability to pull off so many details was an impressive feat that would make any new bride feel safe in the arms of a husband who can lead in a complex situation with such ease.

Be People Sensitive

You should talk ahead of time to determine if your soon to be fiancée would like friends and family to be a part, or nearby soon after the proposal. A lot of couples enjoy having those they love join them for a celebration. As part of your planning, consider the following examples:

- Sixty family and friends were recruited to create a music video proposal.

- An entire choir that the groom and bride were a part of boarded a subway to sing a proposal.

- A sorority house had a tradition of passing a candle to

signify that a woman had been proposed to. When the candle reached the love of one man's life, he entered the room to make the proposal.

- At the curtain call, a boyfriend arranged with his girlfriend's theater company to propose on stage at the conclusion of her play.

- One young man proposed at the top of a mountain path. He then walked his fiancée down the path where she received roses from various family members who had secretly been stationed along the way.

Often a couple will have their moment (on a balcony, a beach, a lakeside dock, or a park), and then return to a gathering of family and friends for a celebration. Every couple has their desires of how private or public they want their moment to be, so it is important to know the heart of the one you love. Regardless of what you choose, we think the incorporation of family and friends is a healthy option. Your marriage will unite two families, so there is value in bringing the families together early in the process.

Pulling It Together

In the spaces below, write down your thoughts on who you would like to have involved in your proposal.

His thoughts:

Her thoughts:

Be Present Savvy

Some suitors will give a simple gift to seal the deal while others will want to make a statement of their undying love by dropping some serious cash. For these guys, the ring is simply not enough. For example, mysterious sand-art was spotted at Ocean Beach, California. An elaborate pattern contained the words, "Will you marry me Kelly?" The sand imprint was created by artist Andres Amador, who was commissioned by Jason Fordley, who might earn a "most romantic man" title if there were such a thing. The elaborate proposal was directed to Kelly Riplinger, who saw the huge message when the couple climbed to the top of a nearby hill. Fortunately, she said yes. The proposal was followed by a city tour, dinner, and a beach party with their friends.[2] The photo of this grand work of art will inspire lovers for years to come.

Other gifts often reflect the personality of the couple—and are more affordable!

- Dave Mosher and Kendra Snyder are both science journalists, so Dave called Kendra to the relativistic heavy ion collider of the Brookhaven National Laboratory to check out a possible story about a strange crystal. She was taken inside the particle accelerator, which was offline for maintenance, where she found out the mysterious crystal was a diamond engagement ring.[3]

- Matt decided that the best way to propose to his girlfriend was through a movie trailer because their love story is "making the movies jealous." He recruited family and friends to help. Ginny thought she was simply going to a movie. At the perfect time, Matt ran into the theater to pop the question.[4]

- If you are a techie, use it to your advantage. One man created an instructional video for a smartphone with the proposal built in. Another created a game that launched the proposal when his girlfriend reached a certain level. Still another used a digital version of Pictionary to create a card where the clues added up to a proposal.

- If you like the outdoors, you may want to create a geocaching adventure or a car rally where clues are coordinated through a GPS-type app that has you revisiting romantic spots and ends with the proposal.

- If you are versed in social networking, you can create a proposal on Twitter, Instagram, Buzzfeed, or a personalized website. Just remember these public displays of affection can be viewed by family and friends—but also by strangers.

An elaborate proposal is commendable if your motives are right. If you are creating a movie to build your career rather than your marriage, you've gone off track. If you are spending vast amounts of money to "prove" your love, your relationship is probably on shaky ground. A good test is to ask yourself, *Am I willing to spend this same kind of energy to build our future marriage, our family, and our walk with God?*

Also keep a safety-first attitude. One man took his girlfriend to a rock known as Proposal Rock. Unexpectedly, a wave came up and swept her out to sea. While a romantic setting is nice, make sure all parties involved—you, your fiancée to be, friends, and family—will all be safe.

Purposefully Celebrate It

If family and friends were not present at the engagement, hosting an engagement party where close family and friends gather to celebrate the couple is a nice way to rejoice. Invite people who are close to you and will likely attend the wedding, but don't feel like you have to invite the entire wedding invitation list. Usually this is a smaller gathering of best friends and family who have been a significant part of your lives.

Traditionally the bride's parents will host an engagement party, but it is not unusual today for the groom's parents, both families, or the couple themselves to host the celebration. With couples falling in love from various geographic locations, sometimes both sets of parents will want to throw a party, or the couple might travel to both hometowns early in their engagement to celebrate with family and friends. The food can be simple, and the announcement of the exciting news should come early in the party. Tell the story of the proposal and give all the guests plenty of time to rejoice and communicate their best wishes.

This is a wonderful time to use your family traditions, culture, and uniqueness to envelop your beloved into the family circle. Our family incorporates a prayer walk, or a prayer circle, so the couple launches into love under the umbrella of God's favor and blessing with a covering of prayer. Other families us this time to pass along a practical gift of wedding help. They may offer to pay for a wedding planner or provide a wedding organization and etiquette book. Others may choose to pass on a family heirloom or propose a toast. Invite those close to you to share a gift of words, prayers, or a tangible gift, if they so desire. Give them an opportunity to speak or have a private moment with the two of you. Talk to important family members ahead of time so they feel included and relationships are built.

Be sure to have some quiet moments together as a couple at the proposal and at the engagement celebration. Once the music and fanfare are over, it will be just the two of you. Look at the proposal and the surrounding activities as an opportunity to enhance your budding love at this early stage of your journey together.

Pulling It Together

In the spaces below, write down your thoughts on how you would like to celebrate your proposal.

Would I rather have a crowd of our family and friends involved at the time of our proposal or do I want it to be just the two of us?

His Response:

Her Response:

After the proposal, do we want to celebrate with a crowd of family and friends, a small group of family and friends, or do we want to celebrate alone?

His Response:

Her Response:

Are there any family traditions we want to incorporate into our proposal and celebration?

His Response:

Her Response:

It Is a Big Deal

Too often, couples get apathetic or listless when headed toward marriage. We were speaking at a "seeker sensitive" church for a marriage conference. As an icebreaker, the meeting planner set up a game where couples would mix and mingle, asking and answering various questions about love and relationships. The question assigned to us was, "How did you propose?"

We thought we might hear some incredibly romantic stories. However, as we asked couple after couple, we were surprised how many had the same answer. They would blush a little and give each other a "do we tell the speakers the real story?" look. Then one would dive in with, "We are kind of embarrassed. It really wasn't very dramatic or memorable. We were lying in bed together (after having premarital sex), and I rolled over and said, 'So, do you want to get married or what?'"

Our hearts broke for these couples. Many didn't even want to tell their children their proposal story. I (Pam) turned to Bill and said, "Thank you for making our proposal story so precious. Thank you for putting so much thought into how you would ask me to be your wife. I am so proud to tell our love story to our kids and grandkids and to anyone who will listen."

Our Story

Pam: Prior to meeting Bill, God lead me to take a dating sabbatical. For one year I worked on falling in love with Jesus instead of falling for every ambitious man who came along. Focusing on my Savior trained my senses to recognize healthy men who reflected the kind of love I saw in Jesus' life. I saw Christlike character and love in Bill, who had been serious about his relationship with God since it began in high school. I was his first Christian girlfriend, and I could tell he wanted to do things right.

We wanted to do things God's way, so we dated very intentionally. We were aware of our weaknesses (intensely focused on goals, aggressive in our pursuits, and wired "hot"). If we lit even the beginnings of passion, we knew our hormones would fan the flame and ignite a forest fire of desire. Guarding our hearts and future became a premium value, so we decided we would not kiss on the lips until we got engaged. We might do a quick kiss on the check, as you would greet a brother or sister, but typically a big bear hug was how we said hello and good-bye. We would hold hands or walk arm-in-arm, but we were set on making it to the altar sexually pure. This was a radically different choice from most of our peers, but we were convinced it would create a strong foundation for the kind of marriage we wanted.

Bill: After dating for six months, we decided to test our relationship.

Pam was attending a summer Bible school while I was heading home to work. We decided not to write or talk on the phone during this time. We agreed to pray and ask God if we were "the one" for each other. If we didn't really miss each other, we would free ourselves to pursue God's path and a different partner. If our time of separation and prayer drew us to each other, I would consider that a green light to move toward a proposal for marriage. We decided to meet at a certain restaurant on a certain day at a certain time, just like a script out of a romantic movie. I can still remember the feelings of anticipation and trepidation.

Pam: So on a beautiful, warm evening in August of 1979, Bill said, "Would you like to share what God revealed to you first, or would you like it if I shared first?" Wanting to acknowledge Bill as the leader in our relationship, I replied, "You go first." He told the story about how he was convinced God wanted him to marry me.

Bill: I told Pam that as I had driven home at the beginning of summer, I had a long argument with God. *Lord, I am too young. I haven't finished my degree. I own two pairs of pants, and one of them has hole in the knee. I can't get married.* As I prayed this way, I had a painful knot in my stomach. I would then give in and say, *Okay, God! I'll marry the girl.* I would feel an instant sense of peace, but it was too hard to accept, so I would begin to argue again. *I drive an old car. I work at a gas station. I have no savings. I can't get married!* The same painful stress would reappear. It took me two hours to resolve it, but I finally said, *God, I cannot argue with you anymore. I am nervous about this, but I am committing to marry Pam and trust that everything will work out.*

Pam: Then I shared my story of how God had led me to be ready to say yes to a proposal from Bill. I was at the Institute of Biblical Studies in Colorado and surrounded by godly young men, so I honestly wondered if Bill was the one. On the last afternoon before returning to meet up with Bill, I realized I only wanted to talk to and about Bill.

After sharing our stories, we were both excited that God had confirmed the call to marry each other. We had decided ahead of time that the actual proposal would come after this night, just in case God was leading us apart. I didn't want Bill to buy a ring he wouldn't be using!

After hearing how God had given a green light to both of us independently, we were thrilled that God was merging our lives.

Bill: Knowing that we were going to spend the rest of our lives together raised two pressing questions: (1) How would I propose to Pam, and (2) How long would our engagement last? Even though I wanted to kiss Pam that night, we had made a vow before God not to kiss until I proposed, so I remained patient. I put plans in place, but I had a strategic question for Pam: "Do you want to help choose the ring?"

Pam: I wanted my future husband to select the ring with some input from me. Be sure to check with your love because most women have an opinion about whether they want their lover to choose the ring or if they want to choose it together. We looked at a few rings, so Bill had a rough idea what I liked, but the final selection was his.

Bill: At the time, I was living in San Louis Obispo along the California coast. Many of our most meaningful moments, conversations, and romantic dates had happened in that city. So I planned the special day to include time at the beach followed by a romantic dinner in town. After the meal, we walked, talked, laughed, and dreamed. We then stopped at the condominium I was living in, which had been prepared by my roommates. I sat Pam in a chair next to a table decorated with a bouquet of flowers.

Pam: He then got down on one knee and began to sign a song he had written just for me, which surprised me because Bill isn't known as a singer.

"Stay with Me"
Stay with me
Stay with me
Come and live your life with me
Together we can rearrange our plans

We can dream our dreams
And we can make our plans
And we will make them work just you and I

…If you will

Stay with me
Stay with me
Come and seek our Lord with me
Together we'll become two into one

We'll pray by our choice
And we'll listen for His voice
And He'll lead us to
The greatest life there is…

…I want you to

Stay with me
Stay with me
Come and give your love to me
You are to me what no one else could be

You light up my life
And you treat me like a king
Apart from you
I don't want a thing

…But to

Stay with you
Stay with you
I want to give my love to you
And be to you what no one else could be

I'll treat you like my queen
You're the most beautiful girl I've seen
I love you now and I always will

…So won't you

Stay with me
Stay with me
Come and live your life with me
Together we'll become two into one

At the end of this ballad, Bill said, "Will you stay with me, Pam? I believe God has called us together. Would you do me the honor of being my wife?"

"Yes!" I replied enthusiastically.

Then he asked, "Can I kiss you?"

And before the word *yes!* was completely off my lips, our lips met in that long-awaited, very passionate kiss. It was well worth the wait!

Bill then handed me the framed lyrics to "Stay with Me," and he had also recorded himself singing the song so I could play it over and over and over (which I did).

Bill: I wasn't able to give her the ring that day as I was a struggling college student. I was working to pay it off so the jeweler would release it.

Pam: So our three-part proposal was finalized a few weeks later in the library of the ministry Life House where we fellowshipped weekly. Bill got down on one knee and said, "I have a gift to seal our decision. Pam Rogers, I believe God is calling us to serve him as a team. Will you still marry me?" And of course I said, "Yes!" We kissed and prayed, cementing our commitment to head to the altar.

We immediately phoned our closest family members. We then announced the decision to our mentors and best friends, who were arriving for a ministry leadership meeting. It all seemed so natural and so fitting considering we have served God as a team since the day we first believed God was calling us to be a couple.

Bill: This was all exciting, but we still had to decide how long we would be engaged before we said, "I do." I thought I had good reasons to wait for a while, which included:

- Pam and I still had two years of college to complete.
- Neither of us made very much money.
- We were only twenty years old.

As we talked, however, the following thoughts began to dominate our conversations:

- We believed God had called us together.

- We were very much in love, and it would be hard to wait to engage in sex with each other.
- We lived in different towns, and our relationship would be much easier if we lived in the same town.
- We were hard workers and were willing to do whatever it took to build careers and finish our degrees.

We finally concluded that we needed to have an engagement that was just long enough to effectively plan a wedding. As a result, three and a half months after the proposal, we were joined as husband and wife. It was challenging at the time, but looking back we are really glad. We figured out our careers together, our finances together, our goals together, and we learned how to say no to things we didn't need. It was a great laboratory for learning how to trust God and prepare for the selfless realities of family life.

DATE *to* DISCOVER

Host a dinner party to which you invite three to five married couples. Over dinner ask them each to share their engagement stories. Afterward, talk about what ideas you especially liked and which ones you don't think would fit in your relationship.

A Little Adam & Eve Humor

A little boy opened the big family Bible. He was fascinated as he fingered through the old pages. Suddenly something fell out of the Bible. He picked up the object and looked at it closely. What he saw was an old leaf that had been pressed between the pages.

"Momma, look what I found," the boy called out.

"What have you got there, dear?" his mother asked.

"I think it's Adam's suit!"

8

What Will Our Wedding Day Be Like?

Make a Memory You Treasure Forever

May the saddest day of your future be no worse
Than the happiest day of your past. [1]

$\mathcal{P}$lanning your wedding ceremony is one of life's greatest experiences. Some of the elements of your wedding will be similar to others, but your ceremony will be a unique reflection of who you are as a couple. It makes sense, therefore, to spend time designing your ceremony.

The time and effort you put into planning your wedding will make it one of those days you will talk about for the rest of your life. As you think about your big day, consider what some other couples had to say about their celebration:

- I loved every minute of the rain…It started to rain in the middle of the ceremony, right when I was starting to say our vows. We looked at each other and laughed. It made the day far more special than it ever could have been. [2]

- For me, I remember hearing the vows Paul wrote for me and thinking that I must be the most special woman on earth…I also remember that it was the first time my cheeks actually hurt from smiling so much! [3]

- My favorite part and biggest recommendation is to DO A

"FIRST LOOK." We did all of our pictures before the ceremony, and it was so nice because (a) my hair and makeup were fresh, (b) we could spend the entire day together after that, (c) we weren't rushed to take pictures after the ceremony while all of our guests were waiting.[4]

- Our ceremony…was casual, moving, and at times totally hilarious. The sense of community was magical and humbling.[5]

- Things will go wrong…[and] people are totally going to notice…There's no *script* at a wedding; you can't plan for every single eventuality, and when the unexpected stuff happens—providing nobody, you know, stands anyone else up at the altar or *dies* or anything—that's when your wedding day becomes an actual, real, jam-packed-to-the-gills-with-life wedding day and not some scene from a Disney movie.[6]

Let It Be You

Planning your celebration begins with the question, "What message do you want your wedding to communicate to the people you are inviting to your ceremony?"

You have invited the most important people in your life to this event. Some you invited because they've made a significant contribution to your life, shared some of your most important experiences, or helped you through a significant transition. Others you have invited because they are attached to your family in a significant way. Since these people are all connected to you, they will remember the overall impression this event leaves even though they won't remember all the details. A wedding ceremony you will be proud of begins with the end in mind. What do you want people to say about your wedding when it is over?

Please do not shortcut this step. So much of wedding planning revolves around the building, the decorations, the flowers, the food, and the clothes. To be sure, these are important, but they easily over-shadow the strength of your love as well as the personal, spiritual commitment you are making to each other. It is common for people to put so much pressure on themselves to get all the details right, they end up being disappointed with their wedding day.

- Kim courageously admits, "Okay, I'm coming clean: I didn't like our wedding reception. I was jealous that our guests had more fun than I did. And most of all, I didn't like who I was on that day…after lots of hard 'inner work,' I came to love our terrible wedding day without necessarily feeling obliged to like it." [7]

- Samantha recalls, "Me being me, I started to worry about things, so many things. I worried about the location. I worried about the food. I worried about flowers and cake and favors…I worried that no one would come. I worried that too many people would come. I worried no one would talk, that we would all just sit in awkward silence staring at each other and silently begging time to go faster so the horrible pain of my boring wedding would stop. I worried and I worried and I worried…So I talked to Mark…We talked about what was important to us. We talked about why he didn't want to elope and I did. I listened to him. He listened to me." [8]

- Anthony confided in Bill, "I love Rachael, but this was a rough day. There were so many expectations and so many demands from the woman I just want to be in love with. I know this day is important, but it's hard to like someone who turns pushy and unreasonable. I'm pretty sure it was just the stress of the day and I'm praying this is not the way it's going to be in our marriage."

Taking time to identify the message you want people to walk away with helps you prioritize everything else and sort through the myriad decisions you will be confronted with. Here are a few examples of what couples have identified as the message of their ceremony:

> We want our wedding to be fun and friendly. We want people to laugh with us, celebrate with us, and feel like they belong. We know it's not really possible, but we would like it if everyone felt like they were on the stage with us, like a big circle of friends.

> We want our ceremony to be God-honoring. We want it to be obvious that we know Jesus and we want him to be the center of our relationship. We want everyone to pray with us, hear our favorite Bible verses, and understand that our love for each other is a gift from God.

> Our ceremony will be a celebration of the legacy that exists in our families. Both of our parents have been married for twenty years or more. All of our grandparents have been married for forty years or more. Both sides of our family talk about couples who have celebrated their sixtieth anniversary. We want everyone to know that our family believes in marriage and that we are committed to being married for life.

> We want everyone to sing with us. We love music and we want lots of it at our wedding. We want special music and songs people can sing along with. We both want to sing to each other during our ceremony.

> A simple ceremony is all we really want. Neither of us likes to be the center of attention, so we would like a traditional ceremony that follows a typical script so there's not too much of a spotlight on us.

As you talk about the theme of your wedding, don't overwork the conversation. This is not a test and it is virtually impossible for you to get this wrong. It's tempting to think long and hard about this so you "get it right." Getting it right, however, is not the goal. This is your ceremony and you should simply want it to reflect the best of who you are. We can tell you from experience that something will go wrong. Fortunately, even the things that go awry can become fond memories over time. Here are some of the more memorable faux pas we have been a part of:

- As the minister prayed for the couple, a bridesmaid kneeling next to Pam blacked out and fell over.

- A friend of ours got so dizzy at the altar that the wedding party had to go to the pastor's office to conclude the ceremony. After a few minutes, the best man came out to announce, "Thank you all for supporting Duann and Angelique. Everyone is doing okay and they are officially married. They will see you all at the reception."

- I (Bill) performed a wedding ceremony with my zipper down!

- At the next wedding I performed, I turned to the men in the wedding party just before we went on stage and said, "Men, check your flies." It was good advice, but the microphone that fed the video camera was turned on so my comment is now an official part of that couple's ceremony.

We could go on, but suffice it to say, something will go wrong and that's okay. You will forget much of what happens on your wedding day, but you will remember the unexpected and you will eventually laugh about it.

Write down the thoughts that come to mind quickly after asking yourselves, "What message do we hope people take away from our wedding?"

It's Your Turn

His: The message I hope our wedding day carries is…:

Her: The message I hope our wedding day carries is…

Ours: Combine your two ideas and create one sentence or paragraph that answers, "The message WE hope OUR wedding day carries is…"

How formal do you want your ceremony to be?

All you really need to do to get married is say "I do" in the presence of someone authorized to sign your wedding license. The rest is a celebration of the love you share for each other. So design the ceremony in a way that fits who you are as a couple. One important consideration is the style of your celebration, which can range from a very casual outside gathering to a very formal traditional ceremony. Review the options below to help you decide how formal you want your ceremony to be.

Very Casual
- outdoor venue
- men wear shorts and a casual shirt
- women wear sundresses
- bride and groom face each other

- lighthearted mood
- focus of the ceremony is on casual stories about the couple

Casual

- outdoor venue or at a home
- men wear casual slacks and shirt
- women wear casual dresses
- bride and groom face each other
- lighthearted mood
- focus of the ceremony is on the couple's journey together

Friendly

- church or other wedding venue
- men wear suits
- women wear semiformal dresses
- bride and groom face each other
- mood is interactive
- focus of the ceremony is on the purpose of marriage and support from friends

Semiformal

- church venue
- men wear tuxedos
- women wear semiformal or formal dresses
- bride and groom face each other
- mood is dignified and responsible
- focus of the ceremony is on the couple and the commitment they are making to each other before God

Formal

- church venue
- men wear tuxedos
- women wear formal dresses

- bride and groom face the minister
- mood is sober and serious
- focus of the ceremony is on the prescribed tradition of the church in which it is held

You may choose to adopt one of the settings described above or you may choose to integrate elements from two or more. On the chart below, mark your preferences and then talk them over with your fiancé(e).

I prefer the following style of ceremony:	Groom	Bride
Very casual		
Casual		
Friendly		
Semiformal		
Formal		

Instead of one style, I would like the following elements to be part of our ceremony:	Groom	Bride
Type of venue		
Style of dress		
Face each other or face minister?		
The mood of the ceremony		
The focus of the ceremony		

Two Really Are Better Than One

It is common for the bride to drive these decisions about a couple's wedding ceremony because she has probably been thinking about it for years. From the time she was a little girl she has dreamt about her wedding day, being swept off her feet as a princess and being the most beautiful woman in the world for at least a brief moment. As a result, she is emotionally invested in this day. It's a good idea, however, for the two of you to talk about these preferences together because it begins to lay a foundation for decision making where strong emotions are involved.

Little boys, on the other hand, dream about being superheroes, winning wrestling matches, and going on adventures. For most boys, being a groom at a wedding was nothing more than a vague idea they heard others mention. As a result, a groom's opinion about his wedding is not well formed or strongly held at the time of his engagement. It is easy, therefore, for the bride's opinions to overpower his. It may not be that big of a thing when it comes to the wedding, but it will be important later when you have to make emotionally charged decisions about finances, children, careers, and time commitments.

John and Stephanie had a great wedding day. It was sunny and warm. Their friends and families were excited to be there celebrating. They seemed to be the perfect couple, perfectly in love and in sync with each other. On this festive day, they could not have predicted the agony they would experience later.

Stephanie had written out her wedding plan when she was fifteen years old. She picked out colors, the style of dresses, the accents for the men's tuxedos, the flowers. Every detail had been imagined and carried in her heart for almost a decade.

John had not thought about a single detail for his wedding day until four weeks before the ceremony. He thought it was cute that Stephanie described her plan with such great enthusiasm, even though he didn't like the idea of the men wearing pink vests with their black tuxedos. His attempts to talk it over with her totally failed, but he concluded it was not that big a deal.

"Stephanie, you have obviously put a lot of thought into this."

"Yes I have. I've been carrying this plan around since I was a teenager. I could see even back then exactly what I wanted my wedding day to be like."

"I love almost everything, and I'm confident it's going to be a great day."

"What do you mean, almost everything?"

"Well, everything is awesome, but I'm not real comfortable with the men wearing pink."

"It has to be pink. It's the only color that will match the women. Besides, it's only for one day, and you guys will look great. In fact, pink is in and lots of men wear pink today."

"I know that, but I'm still uncomfortable. Isn't there any other color we can consider?"

"I can't believe this is happening. It was going to be perfect, but now it's all falling apart!"

Stephanie began to cry. John didn't understand what the big deal was, but he could tell it would be painful to keep talking about it. He decided to give in and just let Stephanie have her way.

John and Stephanie had no way of knowing that this was how they would make decisions later on. When Stephanie feels strongly about something, an intense need to have it turn out her way takes over and makes it almost impossible for her to talk things over or consider other options. After they had their first child, that pattern intensified even more because now a baby's life was affected. Anytime John would discuss important issues with her, she would panic inside. She discovered she was willing to use almost any tactic to convince John that her way was best. She would argue, cry, stall, and give long justifications for her point of view. If those didn't work, she would accuse him of being selfish and incessantly ask for explanations until he gave up and let her decide.

Year after year, resentment built up, and John found himself responding in anger to most of their discussions. They are now working to redefine their relationship so that Stephanie is less controlling and John is more engaged in decisions that are emotionally charged. It's hard work, though. It has been challenging for Stephanie to give John a bigger role when her emotions are trying to convince her she is right. When she yields to his wisdom, it feels to her as if things are going to turn disastrous.

It has also been challenging for John as he learns to be more engaged in decision-making conversations. Together, they decided that he would have authority for decisions about the yard, the cars, and "his time" with the kids. Since these are areas Stephanie cares about, she has an opinion about every aspect of his decisions. When she shares these opinions, his initial reaction is to get angry. Learning to stay calm but firm has been more difficult than he anticipated. It sounds easy when you say, "Hold your ground, stay calm, and compliment her for caring, but do what you believe is best." It is much harder when his beautiful, demanding wife is employing all her persuasive strategies.

Decide *How* You Will Decide

Choosing a process for making decisions about your wedding plans will make it easier to remain unified as a couple. Methods you may want to consider include:

Delegate decisions to a team. Let professionals, experienced friends, and motivated family members handle the aspects of your wedding that are less important to you. We know that "everything" is important, but some of the details are less so and these can be entrusted to others, lowering your stress. The decider can do the research, and then bring back a recommended course of action for you to approve.

Defer decisions to a wedding planner. Hire a wedding planner who will handle the arrangements, with your approval. If you choose this method, be sure to thoroughly check the wedding planner's references. The best way to find a good wedding planner is to ask friends and family who have recently been involved in a wedding. Your venue might also have a wedding planner associated with it, which can be especially helpful. Members of the clergy are often aware of skilled wedding planners in your area, so don't overlook the wisdom and experience your pastor or priest might lend on a wide variety of wedding-day topics. If none of these options provide a solution, you can check the local Better Business Bureau to help you evaluate wedding planners who advertise their services.

Divide decisions between the two of you. If you are up for it, you two can be your own wedding planners as you divide and conquer the list of choices. You each do the initial information gathering, and then bring back to the other a recommended choice to approve.

By talking about *how* decisions will be made and communicating your plan to friends and family, you can minimize hurt feelings or confusion. When the path is clear, the wedding planning can become a fun part of your growing and deepening relationship.

Trust Your Help

Do you have a wedding hostess? The advantage of having a hostess (or coordinator) is that she helps you relax on your wedding day. Myriad details need to be coordinated. A parade of people need to be gathered and organized. There is a schedule to manage that includes emotionally invested participants, opinionated family members, caterers, musicians, photographers, and expensive facilities. Without a wedding hostess, this responsibility will fall on you as a couple. On the day you are supposed to be focused on each other, you will be forced to focus on a long list of distracting details. If your ceremony is relatively simple or if you have a talented friend or family member who is willing to volunteer, this may not be a problem. If your ceremony has a lot of moving parts, it can get stressful in a hurry trying to get everyone in the right place at the right time doing the right thing.

Our advice is to have a competent minister who can run the ceremony from the front and a conscientious hostess who can run the ceremony from the back. That way you can take in the events of the day, stare into each other's eyes, and bask in your love.

Questions You Probably Have Already Thought About

To help you begin a habit of making decisions as a team, talk through some of the most obvious choices for your ceremony. There are lovely and helpful wedding planning books, kits, and organizational systems available. We suggest you look for a system that will help you keep track of it all since we won't try to duplicate here what those resources offer. The rest of this chapter is primarily focused on big-picture issues and critical decisions connected to the actual day of your wedding. Take some time and attend a wedding bazaar or bridal show and expose yourself to the professionals and resources that might be available to help make your day special and memorable.

Your Wedding Party

Ask couples who have been married more than five years, "Who was in your wedding party, and are you still as close to them as you were at the time of the wedding?" Remember that friends might come and go, but you two will be attached to your families for the rest of your lives. Consider carefully the roles your siblings might play in your big day. Next, look at friends and those who have poured into your life to either bring you two together or to help you become the person your fiancé(e) wants to marry.

Your Ceremony

Once you have identified the message you want your ceremony to communicate to friends and family, the challenge is to include elements that help carry this message. The elements that will have the biggest impact are the music, the message, and the vows.

The music sets the mood for your celebration and fills in the silence whenever you move from one spot to another during your ceremony. The most common example is the procession of the family and wedding party. You can imagine how awkward it would feel if everyone walked in without music playing. The ceremony would seem long and boring rather than inspiring, so spend some time thinking about what music you want to include. The general rule is "whenever you are moving, music should be playing."

We suggest you choose music that has meaning for you as a couple. Consider together the following questions to help you narrow your options:

* Do we have a favorite song, perhaps one that represents a significant time or decision in our relationship?

* Are there songs that make us smile or spontaneously start dancing every time we hear them?

- Is there a song that captures the message we want our ceremony to give?

- Is there a musician who is a close friend or family member we want to include?

Special Participants

Certain people in your life may have played a significant role in your growth and development. They were present during important milestones. They were a source of strength and wisdom for your important decisions. They helped you gain confidence and perspective throughout your life. It is an honor for them to be included in some way. If they are members of the clergy, you may want to have them either officiate or co-officiate the service. If not, you may want them to read a passage from the Bible, share a poem, or pray over you as a couple.

Who Will Give Away the Bride?

You're no doubt aware of the traditional method of giving away the bride, which involves the father of the bride walking her down the aisle and, eventually, giving her hand to the man who will be her companion for life.

There is another approach that is used quite often, especially in more informal weddings. Couples who choose this option are motivated by a desire to get more people involved in their ceremony and by a recognition that both the bride's and the groom's families share equally in helping to establish this new family.

In this approach, both families stand after the bride is escorted down the aisle. The person officiating the wedding addresses the groom's family first:

> It is traditional for the father of the bride to give her away. However, in a real sense, both families share in the giving and receiving. Therefore, will you, as (insert groom's name)'s family, not only give (insert groom's name) to be

(insert bride's name)'s husband, but also joyfully receive (insert bride's name) as a new member of your family?

Together, the groom's family responds with an enthusiastic, "We will." The person officiating then repeats the process for the bride's family.

Wow Your Vows

Wedding vows come in two versions. The first is traditional vows that have been used for many years. There are a few variations, but they all guide the loving couple in a clear statement of commitment to each other. Your choice of clergy will have samples of these to select from or adapt.

The second version is vows that you personalize. These are harder to come up with, but we encourage you to write out your own statements of commitment and devotion to each other. This is your opportunity to put your signature on your ceremony. Because these are your personal vows, no one will ever exchange vows exactly like them. They make your ceremony a one-of-a-kind experience. We suggest the following process for writing your personal vows:

Collect Your Thoughts

- Make a list of personal traits you love about your fiancé(e).
- Write down your responses to the question, "When I think about marrying my fiancé(e), what thoughts come to mind?"
- Write down your thoughts to the question, "What do I love about my fiancé(e)?"
- What are our favorite things as a couple? Include inside jokes, special memories, favorite activities, and romantic habits you share.
- Write down your thoughts to the question, "What does it mean to me to love my fiancé(e)?"

Organize Your Thoughts

- Look at the thoughts you wrote down in the exercises above and rearrange them according to topic or similarities. Possible categories include: my attraction to my partner, character qualities I love about my partner, the ways my life is better because of my partner, commitments I want to make to my partner, things in our relationship that make me smile or laugh.

- After organizing your thoughts by categories, string them together in a series of short sentences.

- Take a break for a couple of days and then revise your thoughts while you ask, *Does this sound like something I would say?* The goal is to make these as personal as you can so you want them to sound like you.

We recommend you use both traditional and personal vows. The traditional vows add a sense of honor to your ceremony and ensure that the legal requirements are met. The personal vows add your touch to the ceremony so that it reflects who you are as a couple.

Your Love Rings True

We assume you will exchange rings at your ceremony as a symbol of your love and commitment to each other. Look at the examples of what other couples have said as a starting point to create a statement that captures your true sentiments.

I give you this ring as a symbol of my love and as a promise of the lifelong commitment I have made to you today.

I give you this ring as a symbol of my love for you. Look upon this ring and let it remind you of my love for you at all times, even when I am not near. With this endless circle of gold, I promise you my undying love forever.

With this ring I promise you my love. Please wear it as reminder of my love for you and as an announcement to the world that you are the only woman/man I truly love.

Spiritual Unity

The verse we chose to put on our gifts to each other at our wedding was 1 John 4:19, "We love because he first loved us." The secret of life-long love is a personal, consistent dependence upon God. Everything a couple needs to succeed (such as love, dedication, willingness to selflessly serve, self-control) are provided by God himself to those who are willing to trust in him. It is common, therefore, for couples to include one or more symbolic representations of their dependence upon their Savior. Possibilities include:

Unity Candle

This is the most popular one used by couples because it is simple, elegant, and memorable.

Communion

Many couples choose to take communion during their ceremony. This is a direct statement of a couple's dependence upon Christ and heightens the spiritual emphasis of the ceremony. For most couples, this is a private act and is not extended to the guests. Be sure to check with your minister if you desire to include communion.

Sand Ceremony

This has become a popular addition to many people's weddings because it works well at outdoor ceremonies (as opposed to candles that get blown out easily) and it creates a memento that can be displayed in the new couple's home. It has also become popular for couples who already have children because they can include their children in the building of the sand sculpture.

The purpose of this ceremony is to symbolize the uniqueness of each couple. Just as there has never been another person exactly like you, there also has not been a couple exactly like you. You have a unique combination of traits, interactions, and convictions. In the same way, when you create a sand sculpture together, it will be a unique creation.

The process begins with three large vases. The largest one will be empty while the other two are filled with sand—one color to represent the groom and a different color to represent the bride. The bride and groom take turns pouring their sand into the largest vase. As you go back and forth adding a little sand at a time, a sand sculpture is created in the vase that can never be recreated. It is a unique piece of art created by a unique couple on a unique day.

The Kiss

Most weddings become "official" when the minister says, "You may now kiss your wife." Be sure to discuss what kind of kiss you are comfortable with at this point in the ceremony. Brides, this is a good time to trust your new husband's leadership too.

Your Introduction as a Married Couple

The moment you are announced as a new couple at your wedding is one the greatest moments of your journey together. There are several possibilities of how your minister can introduce you to your family and friends:

> Mr. and Mrs. John Smith (This is the most common)
>
> Mr. and Mrs. John and Jane Smith
>
> John and Jane Smith
>
> John Smith and Jane Johnson Smith

Often additional traditions are implemented here: jumping a broom, crushing a glass, releasing a dove or butterflies. Are there any specific traditions that are part of your family or culture or religious worship that you would like to include as the ceremony closes? Is there a musical choice that best expresses how you feel or how you would like your guests to remember you?

If your love story has a specific "happy ever after" tale, look for a way to incorporate it. If you met at a summer camp, you might decide to get married there. If you are both from a unique cultural background, bring in those cultural traditions. If you are both musicians, sing or play instruments at your wedding. One couple we know are both from cattle ranches, so they remodeled her parent's barn for a purely coun-try-flavored wedding.

Your Reception

The wedding reception can be an extension of your personality and commitments. Think through what you want expressed at the reception too. Here are some questions to ask about your "after the ceremony" celebration:

* How elaborate and substantial do you want the food to be? This is where a wedding can become very expensive. Think through your options and your budget carefully. Too often we see couples put off the wise decision to marry because they can't afford the elaborate reception! The party should *not* be the determining factor in when and how you marry.

* Where will guests sit?

* Will the clergy or a family member pray over the meal?

* Who will give toasts?

* Who will thank the guests for coming?

* What is the timeline for the reception?

* Any other traditions that are a part of your family, culture, or religious expression?

* Will any gifts or tokens be given to guests?

* How will the couple exit?

Be sure to take steps that have the wedding reception express your personality as well as your values and beliefs. Again, a good wedding planner and your minister can help walk you through many of these decisions. Often a reception deejay can walk you through parts of the celebration and provide leadership on the day of your reception.

Be yourself all the way through the ceremony and reception and you will be much more likely to enjoy your wedding day. It will capture who you are as a couple and become the doorway to your new life together.

A Final Note

As you head into your wedding day, do so with a healthy balance of honor and humor. It's going to be a day of memories, smiles, sentimental interactions, and love. Remember, however, something will go wrong on this day. We hope it will be something minor, but it could be as embarrassing as dropping a ring or the minister forgetting your names. (Bill actually did that! Only once, but it did happen.) In the long run, it will be the thing you remember with the greatest clarity and you will laugh about it for decades. It is a healthy reminder that marriage is a serious, lifelong commitment entered into by two consistently imperfect people.

That is the essence of love. Two people with great potential, remarkable talents, and pervasive flaws find each other, accept each other with all their goodness and shortcomings, and vow to support each other in a mutual journey of growth and intimacy. Together you will never be perfect, but you will be better together than you could ever be on your own.

Preparing Your Heart

There are lots of resources to help you plan the details of your wedding. The part of the day that tends to get neglected is the preparation of your heart. The wedding is the event that launches a lifelong journey between you, your spouse, and your Savior. The goal of the wedding is to put this connection you have with one another on display in a public affirmation of your dedication. It makes sense, therefore, to engage in activities that keep your heart soft toward each other and toward God.

Set Aside Time to Pray Consistently with Each Other

The weeks before your ceremony are going to be hectic. Stress will rise as you seek to flesh out your expectations for your big day. Praying together can lower this stress, but the pressures of the planning often squeeze out this vital activity. It is wise, therefore, to make an appointment each week to pray together over your new life. If you make it the same time each week and treat it like an appointment, you will see a noticeable calmness invade your heart. You don't have to pray for a long time to stay connected. Five minutes a week every week will be a great reminder of your strength as a couple.

Go on a Date Every Week During Your Engagement

You will be tempted to think you need to spend all your free time working on the wedding arrangements. There is so much to do that you could easily fall into this trap. But you didn't get engaged so you could be event planners together. You are in love with each other. You believe your relationship has what it takes to build a life together. You are becoming intimate partners. It makes sense, therefore, to make the growth of your intimate connection as important as the planning.

Have Lunch with Three Couples You Respect During Your Engagement

Choose couples who have been married for five years or more and whose marriages appear to be strong. Over lunch ask them the following questions:

- What have you done in your marriage that you would recommend to us?
- What have you done that you would never do again?
- What advice do you have for us on our wedding day?
- What advice do you have for us on our honeymoon?
- How do you work through conflict?
- What consistent habits do you practice that keep you connected as a couple?

Plan Your Wedding Night Together

We hope you have waited until your wedding night to enjoy sexual intercourse together. It is one of the most thrilling, personal, and spiritually honorable times you will ever experience. As a result, you don't want to leave it to chance. Take time to discuss the following questions to clarify how you want to share your bedroom:

- What do you want to wear (before you are wearing nothing)?
- Do you want to pray before, after, or as part of your sexual expression? (God is not surprised or embarrassed by what you are doing!)
- What music do you want to play?
- What kind of lighting do you want?
- What type of foreplay do you want to engage in?

Many couples find it helpful to read ahead of time a book on the sexual relationship in marriage, such as *Red-Hot Monogamy* (written by us), *Sheet Music* by Kevin Leman, *Intended for Pleasure* by Ed and Gaye Wheat, or *The Act of Marriage* by Tim and Beverly LaHaye. You can use the suggestions in any of these books to help you decide how you want to approach your intimate expression of love. Even if you have had premarital sex, planning for your wedding night and honeymoon will elevate the value of sexual expression within your marriage. Reading books on this topic can help you heal from past mistakes or hurts. Take time to cherish you marital sexual love.

Most couples look forward with anticipation to enjoying sex on their wedding night, but since the day may well be emotionally and physically exhausting, please do not feel undue pressure. Nobody is keeping score and no one is going to check to make sure you followed through. If you choose to wait until the next morning to initiate sexual intimacy, rest assured you will have joined a club of other loving couples whose marriages are functioning just fine. The key is to decide together so your wedding night becomes a shared memory.

Go on a Honeymoon

Your engagement period is an intense time of planning for a major event. It will be a lot of work and it will stretch you to your limits. You need some time afterward to recover and connect to each other in a relaxed environment.

The fun you will have on your honeymoon and the time you will have to talk about whatever topics come up will create a good foundation to build upon as you merge your lives together. Where you go is not nearly as important as the fact you go together.

We believe you ought to go to a place that is not all that busy. This is not the time in your relationship for sightseeing or heavy social activity. It is a time to get to know each other, to look for your sexual rhythm, to get used to going to sleep and waking up together, and to initiate healthy habits you will practice as a couple. There will be plenty of time in the future for trips to amusement parks. Take jetlag into account since exhaustion is a deterrent to a great time sexually!

DATE *to* DISCOVER

Go shopping together for the outfits you will wear on your wedding night. You may want to buy an outfit you wear in public and then take off each other at the end of the night. You may want to buy lingerie for her and pajamas for him. Choose everything together from underwear to socks to outer garments. It is a great time to learn about each other's preferences and to build anticipation.

A Little Adam *&* Eve Humor

After a few days on the newly created Earth, the Lord called to Adam and said, "It is time for you and Eve to begin the process of populating the earth, so I want you to kiss her."

Adam answered, "Yes, Lord, but what is a 'kiss'?"

The Lord gave a brief description to Adam, who took Eve by the hand and took her to a nearby bush.

A few minutes later, Adam emerged and said, "Thank you, Lord. That was enjoyable."

And the Lord replied, "Now, I'd like you to caress Eve."

And Adam said, "What is a 'caress'?"

So, the Lord again gave Adam a brief description, and Adam went behind the bush with Eve. Quite a few minutes later, Adam returned, smiling, and said, "Lord, that was even better than the kiss."

And the Lord said, "Now, I want you to make love to Eve."

And Adam asked, "What is 'make love,' Lord?"

So, the Lord again gave Adam directions, and Adam went again to Eve behind the bush, but this time he reappeared in two seconds.

And Adam said, "Lord, what is a 'headache'?"

Your Motivation Style

Resources to Consider

𝒜 large body of information is available on the basics of how people are motivated based on their temperament. You may be able to identify your motivation style intuitively, but there are self-assessments you can take to help you hone in on the motivational makeup of your relationship. Resources you may want to investigate include:

Wired That Way. This popular assessment tool by Marita and Florence Littauer includes the time-tested, popular Personality Profile. The Littauers identify the four basic temperaments as Choleric (powerful), Sanguine (popular), Phlegmatic (peaceful), and Melancholy (processer). You can find Wired That Way resources at http://classervices.com/shopsite _sc/store/html/page1.html.

Gary Smalley Personality Types Inventory. Developed with John Trent, this approach presents the four basic temperaments as animals: Lion, Otter, Retriever, and Beaver. A simple assessment is available at http://www3 .dbu.edu/jeanhumphreys/SocialPsych/smalleytrentpersonality.htm.

DISC. This is another popular assessment that presents the four personalities as Dominant, Influential, Steady, and Compliant. A simple assessment is available at www.123test.com/disc-personality-test/.

Wedding Day Devotional

*C*ongratulations! This is your wedding day and it will be one of the most memorable experiences of your life. God is smiling on you today and will be rejoicing with you as you commit your heart and life to the one you love. As you prepare your heart for this important day, read the verses below as reminders of just how interested God is in your future together.

Jesus believes in marriage so much he performed his first miracle at a wedding. Read John 2:1-10 and marvel that if Jesus were attending your wedding today, he might honor it with an amazing surprise.

> On the third day a wedding took place at Cana in Galilee. Jesus' mother was there, and Jesus and his disciples had also been invited to the wedding. When the wine was gone, Jesus' mother said to him, "They have no more wine."
>
> "Woman, why do you involve me?" Jesus replied. "My hour has not yet come."
>
> His mother said to the servants, "Do whatever he tells you."
>
> Nearby stood six stone water jars, the kind used by the Jews for ceremonial washing, each holding from twenty to thirty gallons.
>
> Jesus said to the servants, "Fill the jars with water"; so they filled them to the brim.

Then he told them, "Now draw some out and take it to the master of the banquet."

They did so, and the master of the banquet tasted the water that had been turned into wine. He did not realize where it had come from, though the servants who had drawn the water knew. Then he called the bridegroom aside and said, "Everyone brings out the choice wine first and then the cheaper wine after the guests have had too much to drink; but you have saved the best till now."

Jesus believes what you are doing is a great thing! As you read the passages below, notice how many times your love is referred to as one of the most valuable parts of life.

> May your fountain be blessed,
> and may you rejoice in the wife of your youth.
> A loving doe, a graceful deer—
> may her breasts satisfy you always,
> may you ever be intoxicated with her love.
> (Proverbs 5:18-19)

> A wife of noble character is her husband's crown…
> (Proverbs 12:4)

> He who finds a wife finds what is good
> and receives favor from the LORD.
> (Proverbs 18:22)

> A wife of noble character who can find?
> She is worth far more than rubies.
> Her husband has full confidence in her
> and lacks nothing of value.
> (Proverbs 31:10-11)

Jesus thinks weddings are a big deal. This is such an important theme that our entrance into eternity is pictured as a wedding ceremony. Jesus is the groom. All the redeemed are together as the bride. The bride takes time to prepare herself, the groom waits in anticipation, and the crowd rejoices. That same joy will be yours today as Jesus applauds your love.

> Then I heard what sounded like a great multitude, like the roar of rushing waters and like loud peals of thunder, shouting:
> "Hallelujah!
>   For our Lord God Almighty reigns.
> Let us rejoice and be glad
>   and give him glory!
> For the wedding of the Lamb has come,
>   and his bride has made herself ready.
> Fine linen, bright and clean,
>   was given her to wear."
>   (Revelation 19:6-8)

Jesus, thank you that you believe in marriage. We are excited that today has finally arrived and we get to commit to a lifelong journey with each other. We are thrilled to know that you rejoice as we commit ourselves to each other in a lasting marriage. Please cause our love to grow each and every year and use our love to inspire others. In your name, amen.

 Love Chat

We encourage each of you to write a letter to Jesus on the day of your wedding. You can read this to each other on your honeymoon or first anniversary, and in the years to come.

Dear God…

When It's Time to Say "Good-bye"

*A*s you explore questions related to your relationship, you are going to reach a conclusion. Your confidence may go up, which will make the thought of saying "I do" even more rewarding. If that happens for you, congratulations!

It's always possible, though, that you may conclude marrying this person is not a good idea after all. You may discover habits that you can't live with for the long haul. You may uncover attitudes that didn't seem big when you were dating, but now that you are considering marriage, they are deal breakers. You may come to realize your individual approaches to life are really not compatible.

There is no shame in this. Lifelong love is a risky, courageous step— maybe the boldest decision you will ever make. You can't predict everything that will happen, but you must have sufficient confidence in the relationship. The motivation you need to make a commitment to one person for the rest of your life must be clear and without reservations. If you determine that this is not the right person, it is better to set both of you free than to force things out of guilt, social pressure, or a false sense of duty.

If you are faced with this decision, we know it is probably traumatic for you. You may be afraid of disappointing family members. You may be ashamed because of financial commitments you have made. You may be scared you are going to be single for the rest of your life. You may be embarrassed and don't want to admit to yourself or your friends that you made the wrong choice. These are difficult, but they are not reasons to go through with a marriage to someone you know is not good for you.

There is no easy way to navigate these waters, but it will help if you have a plan. Breaking up is a highly emotional experience, so it may be hard to "think on your feet" as you talk. Emotions respond to our decisions, however, so if you put together a plan to follow, your emotions will be more under your control. To help you in formulating your plan, consider including four steps that will help you STOP the relationship.

State clearly the value this person has added to your life. Then explain as simply as possible that you want to cease pursuing the relationship. Don't beat around the bush. The person should clearly know that you want to end the relationship as it currently stands. They should also clearly know they are valued by God and are a valuable person, but they are just not the best fit for you. Often good people are just not good together.

Tactfully handle the other person's feelings. Explain that you know this is difficult and that it is not your intention to cause hurt or pain. This is probably the trickiest part of the breakup because they may use strong emotional appeals to get you to change your mind. You want to acknowledge their emotions without accepting their feelings as reasons to return.

Openly explain the issues. It's only fair that you explain why you think this relationship isn't working. Sometimes a little training or counseling can prepare someone for a future relationship with another person, and God might be using you as iron sharpening iron to better equip this person for more healthy relationships. It is also important that you grasp the issues for your personal growth and your personal resolve to move forward to a healthy life.

A little caution is in order here because you want to be open but not intimate. You have spent significant time with this person, so it is easy to get into a deep conversation about the deficiencies and struggles of your life, which would not be appropriate. Openness means admitting there are unresolved issues without going into details. Intimacy would mean exploring the details in an attempt to reconnect.

Prepare the new plan. You are going to experience intense emotional reactions because you had so much invested in this relationship. You may feel relief, disappointment, and loneliness. You may grieve over the loss of the life you thought you were going to have. You may be consumed with thoughts of the person you almost married. These intense emotional responses are normal when you change course this significantly. Left unchecked, these feelings can fool your heart and cloud the issues of incompatibility. You need a few months to regroup with a plan that ought to include:

- *Dedication to work or school.* Personal independence needs to be reestablished, which is helped by deliberate focus on productivity at work or dedication to your educational pursuits.

- *Increased time with friends.* You will experience a void in your social life, and you will need to reestablish your identity as a single person. Attending a peer Bible study, having lunch with friends after church, and participating in social outings with your peer group are all safeguards to your heart during the transition period.

- *Doing something you've always wanted to do.* You probably have a hobby, ministry opportunity, travel experience, or family activity that you've set aside for the sake of the relationship. This is a good time to pursue one of these. It will help confirm your decision as it adds value to your life.

- *Honesty with God.* During times of worship and personal prayer, you will experience a variety of reactions. Share all of these with your Savior. Tell him if you are happy, relieved, sad, disappointed, angry, scared, or excited about your future. He can handle whatever you are feeling, so be courageously transparent with the one who loves you without limits.

God sees you and has plans for your life. It may not be clear at the moment, but "we know that in all things God works for the good of those who love him, who have been called according to his purpose" (Romans 8:28). As time unfolds, you will see God's good plan for you come together and you will be glad you were courageous enough to wait for his best.

Notes

Chapter 1: Are You Ready for Love?

1. "Toasts to Good Fortune," Etiquette Scholar, www.etiquettescholar.com/dining_etiquette/ toasting_etiquette/toasts_for_all_occassions/good_fortune_toasts.html.

2. "Kids Define 'Love,'" www.greatdad.com/tertiary/295/690/kids-define-love.html.

3. Renee Fisher, *Not Another Dating Book* (Eugene, OR: Harvest House, 2012), 58.

4. Ibid., 64.

5. Chris Matyszczyk, "Get 1 Million Facebook 'Likes' for Sex—and a Puppy," CNET, http://news.cnet.com/8301-17852_3-57564771-71/ get-1-million-facebook-likes-for-sex-and-a-puppy/.

Chapter 2: Do We Have a Strong Enough Friendship?

1. Traditional Irish blessing: www.worldprayers.org/archive/prayers/celebrations/ may_there_always_be.html.

2. For further reading, see Dina Kudasheva, "Chemistry of Love," www.asdn.net/asdn/chemis try/chemistry_of_love.shtml; "Love Molecule," http://xray.bmc.uu.se/Courses/Bke1/1998/ Projects/Lovechem/projekt.html.

3. http://pinterest.com/pin/486670303452375215/.

4. http://pinterest.com/pin/486670303452290993/.

5. Karen Peterson, "Friendship Makes Marriages a Success," *USA Today*, April 1, 1999, http:// lists101.his.com/pipermail/smartmarriages/1999-April/002094.html.

6. "The Kind of Face a Woman Finds Attractive," http://midlife.com/index.php/check-it-out/ laughs-to-share/104-college-study-the-kind-of-face-a-woman-finds-attractive.

7. "Men! Geesh!" http://www.midlife.com/index.php/check-it-out/ laughs-to-share/12294-men-geesh-v15-12294.

8. Adapted from "Laughter Is the Best Medicine," *Helpguide.org*, www.helpguide.org/life/humor_ laughter_health.htm.

9. Ibid.

10. www.demotivation.us/i-never-make-the-same-mistake-twice-1257205.html.

11. http://bukowski.net/forum/threads/intelligent-people-are-full-of-doubts-quote.7039/.

12. Renee Fisher, *Not Another Dating Book* (Eugene, OR: Harvest House, 2012), 31, 50.

13. "This Is How We Met: Renee Johnson Fisher's Story," www.leighkramer.com/blog/2012/02/this-is-how-we-met-renee-johnson-fishers-story.html.

Chapter 3: Are We Compatible?

1. http://alsmusic.com/jokes/wedtoast.htm.

2. Bill Farrel, *The 10 Best Decisions a Man Can Make* (Eugene, OR: Harvest House Publishers, 2010); the five-session DVD curriculum is available under the Products link on our Love-Wise website (http://love-wise.com).

3. Kevin Leman, *The Birth Order Book* (Grand Rapids, MI: Revell, 2009), 18.

Chapter 4: Are We Making Progress?

1. www.searchquotes.com/quotation/Happy_marriages_begin_when_we_marry_the_one_we_love,_and_they_blossom_when_we_love_the_one_we_marrie/385977/.

2. Gary Brainerd, "Stages in Love Relationships," http://relationship-help.com/articlesdetail.asp?id=64&cat=All.

Chapter 5: Can We Handle Our Families?

1. Irish toast, www.goodreads.com/quotes/544831-may-there-be-a-generation-of-children-on-the-children.

2. www.motherinlawstories.com/mother-in-law_jokes_page.htm.

3. One site we have found useful is www.genopro.com, where you can download a free trial, and if you find it helpful, you can purchase the program for a small fee.

4. Sharon Jayson, "Sooner vs. Later: Is There an Ideal Age for First Marriage?," *USA Today*, November 9, 2008, http://usatoday30.usatoday.com/news/health/2008-11-09-delayed-marriage_N.htm, and Steve Watters, "Is There a Magic Age to Marry," *Boundless Blog*, September 14, 2006, http://community.focusonthefamily.com/b/boundless/archive/2006/09/14/is-there-a-magic-age-to-marry.aspx.

5. Glenn T. Stanton, "What Is the Best Age to Marry?" *Focus Findings*, February 2011, www.focusonthefamily.com/about_us/focus-findings/marriage/what-is-the-best-age-to-marry.aspx.

6. Jayson, "Sooner vs. Later."

7. "Knot Now, Americans Say," *Washington Times*, September 6, 2006, www.washingtontimes.com/news/2006/sep/6/20060906-113145-4882r/?page=1.

8. Jayson, "Sooner vs. Later."

9. Anne Reiner, "Cohabitation Harms Marriage, Expert Says," Baptist Press, September 24, 2012, http://www.bpnews.net/bpnews.asp?id=38776.

10. Joe S. McIlhaney and Freda McKissic Bush, *Hooked* (Chicago: Northfield Publishing, 2008), 16.

11. Ibid., 17.

12. Ibid., 31-33.

13. Ibid., 35.

14. Ibid., 43.

15. Ibid., 81.

16. Ibid., 117.

17. Ibid.

18. Marian Wallace and Vanessa Warner, "Abstinence: Why Sex Is Worth the Wait," *Concerned Women for America*, September 5, 2002, www.cwfa.org/printerfriendly.asp?id=1195&departm ent=cwa&categoryid=family.

Chapter 6: How Is Our Emotional Fitness?

1. www.angelfire.com/md/elanmichaels/irishblessings.html.

2. "Money Jokes and Funny Stories," www.transformyourmoney.com/money-jokes.html.

3. Dave Ramsey, "What Does the Bible Say About Money?," https://crc.daveramsey.com/index. cfm?event=dspPastorExt&intContentID=10320.

4. Natalie McNeal, "10 Ways Men and Women Spend Their Money Differently," www.buzzfeed .com/nmcneal/10-ways-men-and-women-spend-their-money-differentl-af9h.

Chapter 7: How Will You Propose?

1. "Classic Wedding Toasts," *About.com*, http://weddings.about.com/od/theweddingparty/a/ toastsamples_3.htm.

2. Mary Jo Bowling, "Sand-Written Wedding Proposal at Ocean Beach," *7x7SF*, April 6, 2011, www.7x7.com/wedding-resource/sand-written-wedding-proposal-ocean-beach.

3. Miss Cellania, "10 Cool and Creative Marriage Proposals," *Mental Floss*, July 19, 2011, http:// mentalfloss.com/article/28272/10-cool-and-creative-marriage-proposals#ixzz2V2ALlq2n.

4. Ibid.

Chapter 8: What Will Our Wedding Day Be Like?

1. "Classic Wedding Toasts," About.com, http://weddings.about.com/od/theweddingparty/a/ toastsamples_2.htm.

2. "Molly Malaney: I 'Loved' That It Rained on My Wedding Day!" *US Weekly*, March 4, 2010, www.usmagazine.com/celebrity-news/news/ molly-malaney-i-loved-that-it-rained-on-my-wedding-day-201043#ixzz2UG6GtVTL.

3. Stacey Martino, "Did You Forget Something on Your Wedding Day?," *Love and Passion Coach* (blog), http://loveandpassioncoach.com/priority/.

4. "Wedding Advice," *Newlywed Moments* (blog), February 27, 2013, www.newlywedmoments .com/2013/02/.

5. "Wedding Graduates: Kim and Brian," *A Practical Wedding* (blog), December 5, 2011, http:// apracticalwedding.com/2011/12/queens-farm-wedding-nyc/.

6. "Things Nobody Tells You About Your Wedding," *Nothing But Bonfires* (blog), September 5, 2011, http://nothingbutbonfires.com/2011/09/things-nobody-tells-you-about-your-wedding.

7. "Wedding Graduates: Kim and Brian," *A Practical Wedding*.

8. "Wedding Graduates: Samantha and Mark's City Hall Wedding and Restaurant Recep- tion," *A Practical Wedding* (blog), May 7, 2013, http://apracticalwedding.com/2013/05/ sf-city-hall-wedding-farallon-restaurant-reception/.

About the Authors

Bill and Pam Farrel are relationship specialists who help people discover how to be "Love Wise." They are international speakers and authors of over 35 books, including the best-selling *Men Are Like Waffles— Women Are Like Spaghetti* (nearly 350,000 sold). A few of their other books include: *Single Men Are Like Waffles, Single Women Are Like Spaghetti; Red-Hot Monogamy; Why Men and Women Act the Way They Do; A Couple's Journey with God;* and *The 10 Best Decisions a Single Can Make.*

Bill and Pam are frequent guests on radio and television, and their writing has appeared in numerous magazines and newspapers. Bill has experience as a senior pastor, youth pastor, and most recently as pastor to small groups. Pam has experience as a director of women, pastor's wife, and mentor. Their books have been translated into over 16 languages. They have been happily married for 34 years and are parents to three children, two daughters-in-law, and three small grandchildren. The Farrels live in San Diego, California.

To contact the Farrels or learn more about their other resources:
www.Love-Wise.com
Love-Wise
3755 Avocado Boulevard, #414
La Mesa, CA 91941
(800) 810-4449
info@Love-Wise.com
Like Bill and Pam Farrel on Facebook
Follow Bill Farrel or Pam Farrel on Twitter

Other Harvest House Books
by Bill and Pam Farrel

Men Are Like Waffles—Women Are Like Spaghetti

Over 350,000 sold!

Bill and Pam Farrel offer biblical wisdom, solid insight, and humorous anecdotes—all served up in just the right combination so that readers can feast on enticing ways to

- keep communication cooking
- let gender differences work for— not against—them
- help each other relieve stress
- achieve fulfillment in romantic relationships
- coordinate parenting so kids get the best of both Mom and Dad

The Farrels explain why a man is like a waffle (each element of his life is in a separate box) and a woman is like spaghetti (everything in her life touches everything else). End-of-chapter questions and exercises make this unique and fun look at the different ways men and women regard life a terrific tool not only for marriage but also for a reader's relationships at work, at home, at church, and with friends.

Also available:

Men Are Like Waffles—Women Are Like Spaghetti Devotional Study Guide

Ideal for individual or group study, small group leaders will find this guide a useful tool for leading couples in biblically based discussions, and couples who choose to go through it together will find the *Men Are Like Waffles—Women Are Like Spaghetti Study Guide* perfect for a create-your-own marriage retreat.

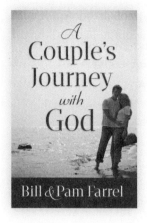

A Couple's Journey with God

Bill and Pam Farrel bring their keen insights into relationships to these devotions that celebrate marriage, encourage open communication, and provide meaningful ways for husbands and wives to draw closer together.

Our busy world often pulls couples apart, but it doesn't have to be that way. Spending time together each day in devotion and prayer will strengthen and bring joy to a relationship as couples learn to connect their love with God's wisdom.

A Couple's Journey with God will expose readers to practical ideas for staying in love, personal tips for great interactions, and passionate prompts for adding that extra spark to their relationship. It's the perfect book for all couples at any stage of life and relationship.

Single Men Are Like Waffles—Single Women Are Like Spaghetti
Friendship, Romance, and Relationships That Work

This specially focused complement to *Men Are Like Waffles—Women Are Like Spaghetti* guides singles through the journey of developing and maintaining healthy relationships with members of the opposite sex. This book offers valuable insight for single men and women as they learn to...

- work together more effectively
- socialize with each other more enjoyably
- date one another more successfully

Discussion topics and activities for small groups are included, as well as a ten-week study guide for couples dating seriously.

Red-Hot Monogamy

With their trademark insight, humor, and candid personal perspectives, Bill and Pam Farrel reveal the truths about the sexual relationship in marriage and what husbands and wives need to know to keep the embers burning.

- *Sex is like fireworks!*—why a little skill turns marriage into red-hot monogamy
- How sex works best spiritually, emotionally, and physiologically
- How to avoid the pleasure thieves that steal your chance for fulfillment

The Farrels present difficult-to-discuss topics and biblical truths in universal language with sensitivity, fun, and understanding.

For newlyweds, golden anniversary celebrants, and all couples in between, this book inspires the gift of romance and passion to fuel lives with love.